# PILANESBERG

CREATED BY JACANA

DISCOVER THE MAGIC

*Jacana*

# Facilities Grid

Black-headed Oriole, see page 22

Dark-capped Bulbul, see page 22

| NAME | CONTACT NUMBER | Game Drives | Game Walks | Bush Braais | Conferences | Disabled Facilities | Curio Shop | Restaurant | Pool | Camping | Self-catering Chalets | Hotel | COMMENTS |
|---|---|---|---|---|---|---|---|---|---|---|---|---|---|
| North West Parks Board | (014) 555-5351 (014) 555-5352 (014) 555-5353 (014) 555-5354 | | | | | | | | | | | | Responsible for biodiversity conservation and tourism management |
| Manyane | (014) 555-6135/6 | • | • | | • | • | • | • | • | • | • | | Caravan park, putt-putt course, aviary and 4x4 track |
| Bakgatla | (014) 555-6135/6 | • | • | | • | | | • | • | • | • | | Children's playground |
| Tshukudu | (014) 552-6255 | • | • | • | | | | | | | • | | Own waterhole |
| Bakubung | (014) 552-6000 | • | • | • | • | • | | | • | • | • | • | Own dam; timeshare and hotel |
| Kwa Maritane | (014) 552-5100 | • | • | • | • | | | • | • | • | • | • | Timeshare; own hide and tennis courts |
| Pilanesberg Safaris | (014) 555-5469 | • | • | • | • | | | | | | | | Also do balloon safaris |
| Mankwe Safaris | (014) 555-7056 083 415 2338 | • | | • | | • | | | | | | | Specialise in heritage drives with particular focus on the Tswana culture |
| Pilanesberg Centre | 083 4412001 083 4539558 | | | | | | • | | • | • | | | Stunning view, sweets, refreshments and clean toilets |

## Acknowledgements

**North West Parks**
Steve Johnson, Hector Magome, Johnson Maoka, Koos Herbst, Bruce Brocket, Phil Johnson, Lowain Van Velden, Gus van Dyke, Les Ashley, Greg Stuart-Hill, Moses Mothusi, Bernard Marobe, Wilf Slade, Doc Shongwe

**Text Development**
Keryn Adcock, Dave Gear (Saint Stithian's College), Dr. John Bristow (Minerals and Energy Policy Centre), Professor Grant Cawthorn (Wits Geological Dept), Simon Hall (Wits Archaeology Dept), Francois Coetzee (UNISA Archaeology Dept), Ria Milburn (Bush Education Safaris)

**Design**
Original design: VIVO Design Associates, Re-design: Lisl Barry

**Artists**
Glynis Clouston, Sally MacLarty, Joan van Gogh, Melanie Wes, Mike Parkin

**Photography**
Paul Funston, Gus van Dyk, Gary van der Merwe

**Translations**
Ephraim Morei, T J Matebesi

**Desk Top Publishing**
Jacana, Anne Centner (Concept Training), Claire Waters, Belinda Bompani, Lana du Croq

**Lithographic Repro**
Three White Dogs, Johannesburg

**Printing**
Fishwick Printers, Durban

**Special thanks**
Clive Webber (Johannesburg College of Education), Val Purves (Golden Leopard), Gert Brummer (Stocks and Stocks Leisure), Glynis & Alistair Clacherty (Clacherty & Ass), Joe Moser (Friends of Pilanesberg), Chris Lee (Friends of Pilanesberg), Rick Matthews, Satellite Applications Centre, Frieda Kilian and the reviewers

**Jacana Team**
Janet Bartlet, Carol Broomhall, Hayley Butler, Paula Correia, Ntokoza Dubazana, Tracey Fisher, Ruth Friedland, Dr Rina Grant, Ingrid Glashoff, Ashwell Glasson, Ruth Longridge, Zandi Luvuno, Joanne Mallet, Obed Molobe, Trudy Musonda, Fortune Ncube, Davidson Ndebele, Janette Ndebele, David Ngwenya, Bambi Nunes, Jenny Prangley, Mariette Strydom, Amanda Thoane, Peter Thomas, Val Thomas.

**aphid** – a tiny insect (bug) that lives on plants, causing them harm

**aphrodisiac** – a substance that arouses sexual desire

**aquatic** – an animal or plant that lives in water

**arid** – an area of insufficient water to support lush vegetation

**bachelor herd** – a herd of male antelope that do not hold a breeding herd territory of their own

**barometer** – an instrument that measures atmospheric pressure

**bosses** – the hard projection on the front of the head or horns of some animals

**breeding herd** – a herd of female antelope in season, kept together by a dominant male that mates with each female

**browser** – an animal that mainly eats leaves

**camouflage** – a method of disguising or concealing animals by their colouring

**carcass** – the dead body of an animal

**carnivorous/carnivore** – an animal that eats meat

**carrion** – the meat of a dead animal (sometimes rotten)

**carrying capacity** – the maximum number of animals an area can hold without causing damage to that area

**catchment area** – an area from which rain drains into a river or dam

**census** – an official count of the animal population

**cere** – the bare coloured skin at the base of bill of a bird of prey

**chiefdom** – an area controlled by one chief

**circumcision** – cutting off the foreskin of a male person, usually as a religious practice

**colony** – birds that breed together in large groups

**conserving** – keeping from harm or loss, for future use

**contour drain** – a man-made furrow which channels water & helps prevent soil wash away

**courtship display** – the behaviour shown by animals while trying to attract their sexual partners

**crust** – the rocky outer layer of the earth's surface

**crustacean** – an animal that has a hard shell

**cytotoxin** – a poison that destroys the body's tissue

**deciduous** – a plant that loses its leaves during winter

**dewlap** – a fold of skin that hangs from the throat of some animals e.g. eland

**diurnal** – an animal that is active during the day

**eco-tourist** – someone who travels to wildlife destinations on holiday

**endangered** – species that are in danger of becoming extinct, & usually protected by law

**engravings** – art that is cut or carved into a hard surface like stone

**excrement** – the waste matter discharged from the bowels

**exoskeleton** – the external bony or leathery covering of an animal

**extinction** – the final loss of an entire species that will never exist in living form again

**fault** – a break in the earth's layers of rock caused by movement of the earth's crust

**forage** – to search for food

**gabions** – rocks that are packed together in wire mesh, in order to prevent soil being washed away

**gape** – the angle at base of bill where upper & lower parts of the mouth meet

**glacier** – a river of ice that moves very slowly

**gradient** – the steepness of a hill or mountain

**grazers** – animals that mainly eat grass & roots

**gregarious** – living in social groups

**habitat** – the natural environment of an animal or plant

**hierarchy** – a system that ranks one animal above another

**indigenous** – plants that are native to an area ie. were not brought in from another area

**initiation** – a special ceremony that admits a person into the society as an adult

**insectivorous/insectivore** – an animal that eats insects

**invasive** – plants that spread easily into an area where they are not wanted

**kraal** – an enclosure for goats, sheep and cattle

**larva** – an insect, from time of leaving egg, until changing into pupa

**latex** – the milky liquid in the stems & leaves of certain plants

**linguistic group** – a group of people who speak the same language

**matriarch** – a female that is the leader of her herd, pride or flock

**migrant** – a bird that moves to warmer areas when it gets cold & food is scarce

**millenium** – a period of 1000 years

**minerals** – non-living material which occurs naturally in the earth, often in rocks

**molten** – rock which has been made liquid by great heat

**neurotoxic** – poisonous or destructive to the nervous system

**nocturnal** – an animal that is active during the night

**nomadic** – people who move from place to place seeking new pasture or hunting grounds

**nursery herd** – a herd of female antelope with young, living together after breeding season

**nutrients** – natural elements which create richer soil

**nutritious** – high quality food

**nymph** – the immature stage of some insects

**ochre** – a yellow, red or brownish mineral made of clay & iron oxide, used as a colouring

**omnivorous/omnivore** – an animal that eats meat & plants

**palatable** – grass which is nutritious

**perennial** – water which lasts all year round

**pheromone** – a chemical substance released by an animal which affects sexual behaviour

**pioneer plant** – the first plants to grow in disturbed soil with very little nutrients

**plumage** – a bird's feathers, particularly in breeding season

**predator** – an animal (carnivore) that hunts & kills other creatures for food

**primate** – a specific type of mammal e.g. monkey, baboon

**proboscis** – elongated mouth part of some insects, used for sucking

**quarantined** – to isolate animals that may be infected with disease

**reservoir** – a source of water

**rhizome** – a modified stem that grows horizontally underground, sending out roots and shoots

**rift** – a deep crack in the earth

**ring-bark** – to cut the bark right around the tree eventually killing it

**riverine** – an area beside a river where the trees are usually evergreen & dense thickets grow

**rodent** – a small mammal that only has cutting teeth & usually lives on plants

**roost** – a place where birds perch or settle to sleep

**sanctuary** – an area where wildlife is protected

**scent-mark** – the way in which animals mark their territories using urine, spray or dung

**scrotum** – the pouch in a male mammal containing the testes

**silting up** – when fine particles of solid matter build up in water & block the flow of water

**smelted** – the heating and melting of rock so as to obtain the metal inside

**solitary** – an animal that generally chooses to live alone

**subcontinent** – a large landmass like southern Africa that forms part of the whole continent

**succulent** – juicy plants that contain a lot of moisture

**tandem** – a situation where animals arrange themselves, one behind the other

**tanning** – to treat the hide of an animal & convert it into leather

**territorial** – an animal that defends a particular area against rivals of its own species (usually the same sex)

**toxin** – a poisonous substance

**trance** – a dream-like state

**translocation** – the moving of animals from one area or park to another

**transpiration** – the act of giving off watery vapour from the surface of leaves

**turbulence** – a state of unrest

**ultraviolet rays** – certain rays of the sun that are harmful to the skin & eyes

**veterinary control** – the control & treatment of animal diseases by a skilled vet

**waterlogged** – areas that become soaked with water after good rains

**weir** – a small dam built across a stream or river, so that water-flow can be controlled

*Crested Barbet, see page 12*

---

## Species Details

### Common Names

The Tswana names of the species, where possible, have been written in brackets.

Tswana is the language of the majority of the inhabitants of the North West Province in the area of Pilanesberg.

### Scientific Names

These Latin names are written in italics below the common names.

### Scientific Data

*Trees & plants*
- Height is measured in metres or centimetres
- National tree numbers are given in brackets

*Mammals*
- Height or length are measured in centimetres or metres
- Height (H) is ground to shoulder
- Length (L) is tip of nose to tip of tail

*Reptiles & insects*
- Length is measured in millimetres, centimetres or metres

*Birds*
- Length is measured in centimetres from beak-tip to tail-tip, or beak-tip to toe-tip (whichever is longer)
- Roberts bird numbers are given in brackets

# PILANESBERG

## A Complete Guide to the Park

This book will give you a broader, and more detailed, insight into the fascinating world of wildlife here.

There is far more to the Pilanesberg than just finding lions!

Pilanesberg is one of the oldest and largest volcanic complexes on earth.

**You may find...**
the largest, or the fastest, or one of the most endangered land mammals on earth; or the largest flightless bird, just one of over 300 species of birds in the Park; or some of the thousands of plant, insect or reptile species.

Of course, one can never hope to see it all, but Pilanesberg's magic will be found in its unique geology, its ancient and extraordinary history, in the diversity of life and in looking for the big game.

One of the best wildlife experiences that you can hope for is waiting for you, if you know where and how to look.

Use this book to help you.

# CONTENTS

## VOLCANOES AND ROCKS

### Birth of Pilanesberg — Pages 2 - 5

These pages take us back 1300 million years, when the volcano erupted. Travelling inside the ancient volcano, you will discover how and why Pilanesberg's geology is so varied and unusual. These pages tie in with the Geological Sites in the Park – see pages 50 - 57. Use the Map on pages 48 - 49.

## FORMATION OF NATURAL HABITATS — Pages 6 - 11

Once the volcano stopped blasting the area into new shape, time slowly started transforming Pilanesberg, and life settled down in this natural sanctuary. The forces of nature gradually changed the landscape and created the habitats we see today. Man-made areas have also been created – dams are now the lifeblood of the Park, and roads have attracted many specific species. The formation of natural and man-made habitats is a never-ending process.

## Contents

# VOLCANOES AND ROCKS

## *Birth of Pilanesberg*

Pilanesberg is one of the largest volcanic complexes of its kind in the world. The rare rock types and structure of the Pilanesberg make it a unique geological feature.

These four pages will take you back into time, to Pilanesberg's violent birth millions of years ago. They explain how it happened and what you can see today, as you drive through the Park.

It is 1300 million years ago. Primitive organisms like algae are the only life-form on earth. It is a hostile place. Strong winds howl, earthquakes and huge volcanic eruptions are common.

**A**

### Tearing the Earth Apart

The furnace inside the earth is hotter than 1000°C and has caused rocks to melt. This molten rock (magma) floods up the cracks the earthquake has caused. The magma collects in a large pool, called a 'hot spot', just below the crust. It builds up immense pressure against the roof of the magma chamber. (Arrows show direction of flowing magma)

**B** **Cracks Release the Fire**

This pressure stretches deep circular and radial cracks to split the earth's crust open. When viewed from above, these cracks look like a window that has been hit by a stone (See Satellite photo, page 5). Boiling rock, ash and gas erupt violently into the sky. The rocks at G1 (see Map, Point 5) are from the initial explosions. They are called volcanic rocks.

**CUT AND POLISHED ROCK SURFACES FOUND AT GEOLOGICAL SITES IN PILANESBERG TODAY**

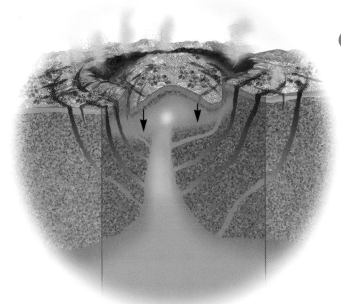

## C
### The Crust Collapses

When the magma bursts out of its holding chamber, there is no longer any support for the brittle, stretched crust above it. As a result, the crust collapses down into the magma chamber. (Arrows show direction of crust collapsing)

## D
### Lava Flows Out

When the crust collapses, magma that is still in the chamber is forced upwards. This process is the same as when a cork is pushed into a full bottle of liquid and the liquid and air spurt out. Magma pours out of the cracks and floods the landscape as lava. This lava solidifies into volcanic rocks and remnants of this can be seen at G3 (see Map, Point 12). (Arrows show direction of lava flow)

## E
### Magma Cools and Clogs Up the Cracks

Some magma does not erupt onto the surface as lava. It begins to cool, harden and clog up the cracks inside the earth. It then solidifies into rock formations known as dykes. They consist of rocks called foyaites and syenites. In Pilanesberg, many of these dykes are circular in shape because of the circular cracks and are called ring-dykes. They are especially prominent in the south-west of Pilanesberg. (See Satellite Photo, page 5)

The entire process happened many times during the volcano's active lifespan of about 1 million years. Each time a new set of cracks opens up, different types of magma are released. Different rock types are formed in this way.

**Eventually the volcano settles down and time and erosion take over to shape the land into what we see today.**

**Key to Rock Surfaces**

Red Syenite · Ledig Foyaite · Red Foyaite · Nepheline Syenite · White Foyaite · Green Foyaite · Kimberlite · Fluorite · Uranium Tuff · Lava · Volcanic Tuff

# VOLCANOES AND ROCKS

## *Birth of Pilanesberg*
### (continued)

### How Erosion Reveals the Secrets Inside the Earth

Erosion has exposed the inside of the original volcano and its rocks to us. Today we see what is left after millions of years of weathering.

### KEY TO GEOLOGICAL SITES IN THE PARK

**Man-made**
Old Flourite Mine G8

**90 Million Years Old**

Kimberlite G4

**1300 Million Years Old**

**Volcanic Rocks**

Volcanic Tuff G1
Lava G3
Uranium-bearing Tuff G13

**Foyaites**

Green Foyaite G6, G10

White Foyaite G5, G14

Red Foyaite G9, G15

Ledig Foyaite G11

Tinguite
No G-site

**Syenites**

Red Syenite G7, G12, G15
Nepheline Syenite G2

**2 000 Million Years Old**

**Pre-volcanic Rocks**

Granite and Gabbro - No G-site

Volcanic rocks (lavas & tuffs) erode much faster than the ring-dykes and outcrops of foyaite and syenite. As a result these erosion-resistant syenites and foyaites stand out prominently.

### Major Rock Types in Pilanesberg Today

Cross Section (indicated by - - - - -) from Sun City (**A**) through Mankwe Dam (**B**) to Manyane (**C**)

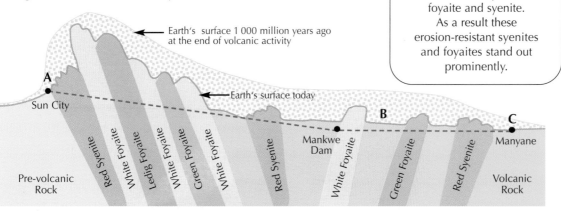

Earth's surface 1 000 million years ago at the end of volcanic activity

Earth's surface today

This satellite photo shows the ring-dyke structure which is more noticeable in the south-west of the complex.
It also shows the central rocky outcrops and flatter regions of volcanic rock in the north-east. Millions of years after the volcanic explosions, a crack in the earth's crust cut the Pilanesberg in half, from the south-west to the north-east.
Erosion took advantage of this weakness and eventually formed a broad valley across Pilanesberg. Tlou Drive follows some of this eroded fault zone.

Mankwe Dam

Thabayadiotso

Fault Zone

Sun City

## KEY

A Tshukudu Lodge

B Bakubung Lodge

C Bakgatla Complex

D Kwa Maritane Lodge

E Manyane Complex

Use the Map on pages 48 - 49 to discover more about volcanoes and rocks. These are at marked Geological Sites (G1 – 15) on pages 50 - 57.

Pilanesberg has survived aeons of erosion and stands high above the surrounding bushveld plains. Near the centre stands Thabayadiotso, which is a fitting name, meaning the 'proud mountain'.

**The turbulence which formed Pilanesberg has moved away long ago, due to the shifting of the earth's continents. For this reason we can be almost sure, that Pilanesberg will never erupt again.**

**But the process of erosion continues and so do the cycles of nature in Pilanesberg.**

# FORMATION OF HABITATS

## *Hillside and Grassland*

Hillside vegetation differs from grassland because the gradient of the slope allows nutrients in the soil to drain to the bottom of the slope. Different soils and the effects of fire also change the vegetation. Grass has relatively little moisture content, and so grassland attracts species which are more dependent on drinking regularly.

### Rain

Water from heavy rainstorms washes soil downhill. Natural erosion is caused, especially on the steeper slopes, where faster flowing water carries away large amounts of soil.

### South-facing Slopes

Southern slopes are cooler and retain moisture, as they receive less sun. Typical trees found here include the Transvaal beech and the cabbage tree.
(See pages 23 & 24)

Flowing water causes nutrients and soil to drain to the bottom of slopes.

### Ouklip

Over decades, as the water from waterlogged areas evaporates, iron-rich minerals are left behind. These bake in the heat of summer. Eventually a hard layer of rock, called ouklip, is formed beneath a layer of top soil. Trees struggle to take root through the hard ouklip layer, but grassland flourishes.

**Ouklip**

### Sweetveld

These lower lying areas become waterlogged in summer. The extra nutrients and water results in the growth of sweetveld. Grazers prefer sweetveld, and it is often over-grazed in summer. As a result, many species move onto hillslopes in winter.

**Sun**

Large rocks are broken down
by centuries of weathering.
Gravity carries them
down the slope.

### North-facing Slopes

North-facing slopes receive
more sun. They are therefore
hotter and drier. As a result
they have different vegetation
from southern slopes.
Some typical trees found here
are the red bushwillow
and the live-long tree.
(See page 12)

Over thousands of years the rocks
are worn down to form soil.
These nutrients in the soil feed
the plants, which in turn
feed the animals.

On grassland animals like zebra,
wildebeest and tsessebe, evolved
in larger herds for two main reasons.

Firstly, grassland provides more food
per hectare than any other habitat and
can sustain large numbers of animals.
Secondly, these animals rely on safety
in numbers, as it is harder for predators
to pick out a single animal from a large
herd. These species developed speed
and stamina to outrun predators
on the open areas.
(See tsessebe page 14)

Two species graze here in smaller
groups – the white rhino which lacks
speed, but is successful due to its size
and strength, and the hippo, which
grazes at night.

# FORMATION OF HABITATS

## *Thickets*

Thickets provide less food per hectare than grassland. Small groups of browsers that enjoy leaves, thorns, fruit, pods and bark, feed here.
Many animals rely on the dense cover of thickets for protection, as well as on camouflage and agility. Small herds can keep together in thickets, even when chased by predators.

Thickets offer safety for mothers and their young. Many species, including the big cats, give birth to young in thickets, keeping them there until they are strong enough to move into more open areas.

## Gully Thickets

Erosion wears away gullies and kloofs between hillslopes. These areas are sheltered from the sun and are therefore usually cooler and wetter.

This gives protection against fire and allows dense vegetation to grow.
Gully thickets are remnants of ancient forests which have survived dry periods due to the shade, protection and greater moisture there.

The safety of taller trees, and easy availability of food, attracts a wide variey of birdlife, especially forest birds.

Browsers gain much of their water requirements from fleshy, succulent leaves. These animals have slimy, thick saliva which helps them deal with plant toxins, rough thorns and bark.

## Termitaria Thickets

Old termite mounds often have trees growing from them. These are known as termitaria thickets. Termitaria are extremely rich in nutrients from the food and excrement of the termites. The channel-ways inside the mound act as a good reservoir for water. Seeds are carried in by wind or birds. The rich, moist soil enables seeds to take root easily here.

**Sun**

**Rain**

After thousands of years of weathering and gravity, rocks tumble down slopes and break up to form soil.

### Break-of-slope Thickets

Vital minerals, nutrients and water collect at the bottom of a slope. This provides deeper soil and more moisture for 'break-of-slope' thickets to grow.

Due to the density of thickets, plants here are protected from extreme weather conditions, especially frost. For this reason plants in thickets are still quite nutritious in winter, and are preferred by many browsers at that time of year.

### Riverine Thickets

Underground and surface streams and waterlines, often result in riverine thickets. In winter, plants keep their nutritional value due to these underground water sources.

# FORMATION OF HABITATS

## *Rocky Areas*

Rocky outcrops in the Park consist mainly of foyaites and syenites. These rocks are harder than most, and therefore do not erode as quickly as other rocks. As a result, Pilanesberg's rocky outcrops stand out prominently. Species, like the klipspringer and leopard, have adapted to this specialised habitat.

Wind, rain, sun, fire and chemical action erode rocks over centuries. This weathering, as well as the force of gravity, eventually loosens large boulders. They tumble down, break up and finally become soil.

Soil, water and minerals flow between rocks, and collect in basins and pockets along the way. At first pioneer plants grow, improving soil conditions. Decaying matter from these plants enriches the soil, so that other more permanent species can grow, later on.

Seeds blown by wind, or carried by birds or animals, come to rest in these fertile, moist pockets of soil. Rocky areas also create favourable conditions for plants to grow by being well sheltered and less susceptable to fire.

Bushveld Red-balloon seed-pod (see Map; Point 30)

Animals in rocky areas are able to climb and jump well. Unlike plain's animals, they are not built for speed. They take advantage of the height and the rocks to avoid predators.

Rocks absorb heat in the day and give off warmth at night. Reptiles bask on warm rocks to regulate body temperature.

Caves and crevices provide excellent shelter and protection from danger.

Most animals that live in rocky areas do not depend on daily water. Their food provides them with enough moisture.

# FORMATION OF HABITATS

## *Dams and Roads*

Man-made habitats have also attracted certain animals and plants.

Dams have given Pilanesberg water all year round and have provided visitors with attractive viewing sites.

Roads are used by many species and they allow visitors to view nature at close range, without damaging or disturbing it.

All streams and rivers in Pilanesberg, arise within the Park itself. They are therefore pollution-free. No rivers here are perennial and they flow only in a wet summer when they refill dams.

Streams from gullies and hillslopes run onto flat areas and natural depressions in the landscape. Some of these natural catchment areas are perfect sites for dams to be built. Dams ensure there is some water during very dry periods.

A smaller dam upstream acts as a filter and prevents the lower dam from silting up. Deposits of silt allow reeds to establish. These also act as a filter and slow down the flow of water helping it to last longer. The result is clearer, cleaner water in the lower dam.

Many animals, especially predators like lions, use man-made roads for easier access. Predators can walk silently here which helps when stalking prey. Roads often stop veld fires from spreading.

Areas with permanent water are well vegetated and therefore attract a diversity of species. Aquatic species, specially adapted to water, live here permanently. These include crabs, fish, aquatic reptiles (like crocodiles and water monitors) and amphibians (like hippos, frogs and terrapins). Dams with islands and dead trees provide safe nesting sites, especially for water-birds.

Water run-off creates dense hedges of vegetation next to the road. However, due to dust thrown up by cars, this is not regularly browsed. These hedges must be controlled by management, to give better visibility to visitors.

## Hillside

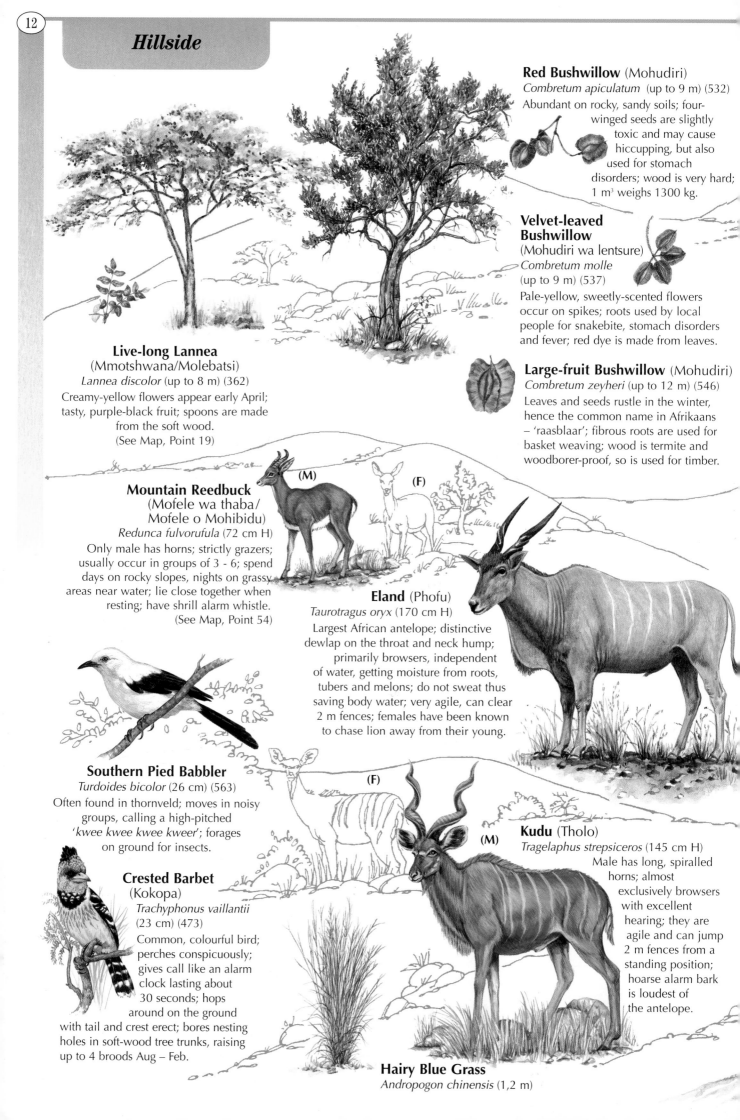

**Red Bushwillow** (Mohudiri)
*Combretum apiculatum* (up to 9 m) (532)
Abundant on rocky, sandy soils; four-winged seeds are slightly toxic and may cause hiccupping, but also used for stomach disorders; wood is very hard; 1 m³ weighs 1300 kg.

**Velvet-leaved Bushwillow**
(Mohudiri wa lentsure)
*Combretum molle*
(up to 9 m) (537)
Pale-yellow, sweetly-scented flowers occur on spikes; roots used by local people for snakebite, stomach disorders and fever; red dye is made from leaves.

**Large-fruit Bushwillow** (Mohudiri)
*Combretum zeyheri* (up to 12 m) (546)
Leaves and seeds rustle in the winter, hence the common name in Afrikaans – 'raasblaar'; fibrous roots are used for basket weaving; wood is termite and woodborer-proof, so is used for timber.

**Live-long Lannea**
(Mmotshwana/Molebatsi)
*Lannea discolor* (up to 8 m) (362)
Creamy-yellow flowers appear early April; tasty, purple-black fruit; spoons are made from the soft wood.
(See Map, Point 19)

**Mountain Reedbuck**
(Mofele wa thaba/
Mofele o Mohibidu)
*Redunca fulvorufula* (72 cm H)
Only male has horns; strictly grazers; usually occur in groups of 3 - 6; spend days on rocky slopes, nights on grassy areas near water; lie close together when resting; have shrill alarm whistle.
(See Map, Point 54)

(M) (F)

**Eland** (Phofu)
*Taurotragus oryx* (170 cm H)
Largest African antelope; distinctive dewlap on the throat and neck hump; primarily browsers, independent of water, getting moisture from roots, tubers and melons; do not sweat thus saving body water; very agile, can clear 2 m fences; females have been known to chase lion away from their young.

**Southern Pied Babbler**
*Turdoides bicolor* (26 cm) (563)
Often found in thornveld; moves in noisy groups, calling a high-pitched 'kwee kwee kwee kweer'; forages on ground for insects.

(F)

**Crested Barbet**
(Kokopa)
*Trachyphonus vaillantii*
(23 cm) (473)
Common, colourful bird; perches conspicuously; gives call like an alarm clock lasting about 30 seconds; hops around on the ground with tail and crest erect; bores nesting holes in soft-wood tree trunks, raising up to 4 broods Aug – Feb.

(M) **Kudu** (Tholo)
*Tragelaphus strepsiceros* (145 cm H)
Male has long, spiralled horns; almost exclusively browsers with excellent hearing; they are agile and can jump 2 m fences from a standing position; hoarse alarm bark is loudest of the antelope.

**Hairy Blue Grass**
*Andropogon chinensis* (1,2 m)

(M)

(F)

## Burchell's Zebra (Pitse e Tilodi)
*Equus burchellii* (136 cm H)
Most common of the 3 zebra species in Southern Africa; black and white stripes have brown shadow lines; no zebra has same pattern; stripes serve as camouflage, with the herd appearing as one unit, which creates confusion for predators; highly dependent on water; formidable fighters, using teeth and hooves.

# SPECIES GUIDE

## *Hillside*

The process of soil formation starts on hills and mountains. This non-living element is the beginning of all life in the Pilanesberg.

Soil, minerals and nutrients that are washed downhill, feed the plants. This sets thousands of food chains into motion… from herbivores, to great cats, to scavengers, and eventually, back to the soil.

Hillslopes provide food for grazers, browsers and mixed feeders. A wide range of species can be seen here. Some of them may be just passing through to better feeding grounds, or moving to a slope with a more comfortable temperature.

## Sable Antelope (Kwalata)
*Hippotragus niger* (135 cm H)
Adult males are darker and have bigger horns; prefer medium-tall grass, drinking water once a day; males are territorial with some in bachelor herds, while dominant cows lead nursery herds; do not usually mix with other animals and most game gives way to them at water.

## Rufous-naped Lark
*Mirafra africana* (18 cm) (494)
Usually seen perched conspicuously, uttering a 'tsee oo' sound, and rattling wings; dipping flight stops abruptly when it drops into grass and runs in crouched fashion, looking for seeds and insects. Also found in grasslands.

## Sabota Lark
(Sebota)
*Mirafra sabota*
(15 cm) (498)
Mimics about 60 other species; usually solitary; forages on open ground for insects and seeds; not known to drink water.

## Gemsbok (Kukama)
*Oryx gazella* (120 cm H)
Graze, but also eat roots, bulbs and melons for moisture; will only drink water when available; sometimes eat the soil for minerals; white belly reflects heat from the bare sand which helps regulate body temperature; kidneys concentrate urine so only a few drops are passed.

## Golden Beard Grass
*Chrysopogon serrulatus*
(1 m)

## Mountain Aloe
(Mokgopha)
*Aloe marlothii* (up to 4 m)
Orange flower heads produce nectar popular with sunbirds; leaves used by local people to make snuff and treat roundworm and sunburn.

# Grassland

## Leadwood Bushwillow
(Motswere)
*Combretum imberbe*
(up to 15 m) (539)
Older trees can be recognised by tall trunk, pale-grey, patterned bark and sparse leaves; small four-winged seeds are pale-green; leaves put on a fire to smoke, will relieve coughs & colds; wood is extremely heavy (1 m³ weighs 1 000 kg); prior to metal, indigenous people used the wood for tools and agricultural implements.

## African Weeping-wattle (Mosetlha)
*Peltophorum africanum* (up to 10 m) (215)
Could be mistaken for a thorn tree as it has feathery compound leaves, but no thorns; bears large clusters of bright yellow flowers throughout summer; pods are flat and long, hanging in dense clusters; spittle-bug nymph feeding on sap secretes liquid froth, hence the tree appears to be weeping; rarely browsed as leaves cause the stomach contents to froth; great ecological value as bacteria on roots release nitrogen into soil.

## Red Hartebeest (Kgama)
*Alcelaphus buselaphus* (1,2 m H)
Conspicuous white patches on rump; can live without water, grazing almost exclusively; when threatened jump stiff-leggedly with all 4 feet off the ground (pronking); very fast animal, can outrun pursuers; mother conceals newborn calf, returning to feed it and eat its faeces and urine which attract predators.

## Tsessebe (Tshesebe)
*Damaliscus lunatus* (1,3 m H)
White on rump is not as prominent as hartebeest; unlike hartebeest, they drink regularly; grazers, preferring grassy areas surrounded by woodland; regarded as the fastest antelope in southern Africa, reaching speeds of 60 km/h; calves join the herd almost immediately after birth.

## Springbok (Tshepe)
*Antidorcas marsupialis* (75 cm H)
Occur in herds; well adapted to hot arid regions as not dependent on water; browse and graze new grass, flowers and bulbs; adults 'pronk' when danger threatens (bound around on stiff legs, backs arched); young copy adults to give vent to energy.

## Black-backed Jackal
(Phokojoe)
*Canis mesomelas* (38 cm H)
Pairs mate for life; males and females defend territory against competitors; efficient hunters, killing young antelope, rodents, hares, birds, reptiles, fish and insects; also eat fruit and berries; follow predators to scavenge.

## Cheetah (Lengau)
*Acinonyx jubatus* (80 cm H)
Prefer open country, have keen eyesight for hunting in daylight; sleek, elongated bodies and semi-retractable claws are adaptations for speed; fastest land-mammal on earth with estimated top speed of about 100 km/h; cubs resemble honey badgers, which possibly deters predators.

## Lion (Tau)
*Panthera leo* (1,2 m H)

Territorial males usually have large manes which develop from 6 months old and serve as protection against bites and blows; lioness does most of the hunting; social animals that observe a strict hierarchy within the pride – adult males often eat first followed by females and cubs; when food is scarce, cubs are unable to compete with adults, often starving to death (up to 80% mortality rate).

## Narrow-leaved Turpentine Grass
*Cymbopogon plurinodis* (30 cm)

## White Rhinoceros
(Tshukudu e Tshweu)
*Ceratotherium simum* (1,8 m H)

Heavier than Black Rhino; mouth wide and square; feeds on short grass in open areas; lives in family groups; poor eyesight but acute hearing and smell; when threatened, put their rumps together facing outwards; newborn calf will follow behind mother, but after a few weeks, it will run ahead.

# SPECIES GUIDE
## *Grassland*

In the wet summer months, water runs off surrounding hills and the flatter savannah areas become waterlogged. This means there will be enough grazing when the season ends. The wide open grasslands invite larger herds of grazers. They have adapted to their environment and are built for speed and stamina to protect them from powerful predators like cheetah and lion. Longer grass helps the hunters but the good visibility of open plains is an advantage to the hunted. Tactics, stealth and speed decide who wins the day.

## Blue Wildebeest (Kgokong e pududu)
*Connochaetes taurinus* (1,5 m H)

Gregarious; territorial males rub facial glands on tree trunks or mark territory on the ground; short-grass grazers, therefore often seen with zebra, impala and giraffe which eat the taller grasses; they also rely on other animals' eye-sight and alertness; pregnant female separates herself from herd to give birth; calves, mobile within minutes of birth, are ready to join the herd within 1 - 2 days.

## Wire Grass
*Elionurus muticus*
(1 m)

# Grassland

## Umbrella Acacia (Mosu)
*Acacia tortilis* (up to 6 m) (188)
Umbrella shape which usually develops a flat crown as tree gets older; whitish pom-pom flowers appear in midsummer; pods, made up of 20% protein, supply valuable food in winter; bark yields edible gum; pods are used to make necklaces.

## Sweet-thorn Acacia (Mooka)
*Acacia karroo* (up to 8 m) (172)
Dark-green, feathery leaves and bright yellow, sweetly-scented pom-pom flowers in midsummer; sickle-shaped pods Apr – Jun; bark exudes an edible gum used in pharmaceutical products; bark also used for tanning leather; flowers produce a great deal of nectar and pollen, attracting many insects; kori bustards are attracted by the gum and the insects; leaves and pods are browsed.

## Lilac-breasted Roller
(Letlekere)
*Coracias caudata*
(36 cm) (447)
Courtship displays are spectacular tumbling aerobatics; hunting from a perch, they seize prey on the ground, sometimes eating it in flight; feed mainly on insects and small vertebrates like lizards.

## Black-shouldered Kite
*Elanus caeruleus* (30 cm) (127)
Can often be seen perched at the roadside flicking its tail up repeatedly, or hovering 100 m above ground and swooping down on rodents, insects, lizards and birds; prey is carried in the feet and eaten while perched.

## Cattle Egret
(Modisa dikgomo)
*Bubulcus ibis* (54 cm) (71)
Acquire red bill with buff plumes on head, back and breast in breeding season; associate with large mammals in open grassy areas, feeding on insects disturbed during grazing; roost near water in the evenings, often flying in 'V' formation.

## Pin-tailed Whydah
(Molope) *Vidua macroura*
(M 34 cm; F 12 cm) (860)
Males are conspicuous, active and aggressive in summer, spending the day chasing other birds; keep about 6 females in breeding season; do not build nests but lay eggs in nests of waxbills and other small birds, relying on the hosts to rear chicks.

**(F)**

**(M)**

## Wool Grass
*Anthephora pubescens*
(1,5 m)

## Snouted Termites (Motlhwa)
*Trinervitermes* species (5 - 6 mm)

## White Buffalo Grass
*Panicum coloratum*
(1,5 m)

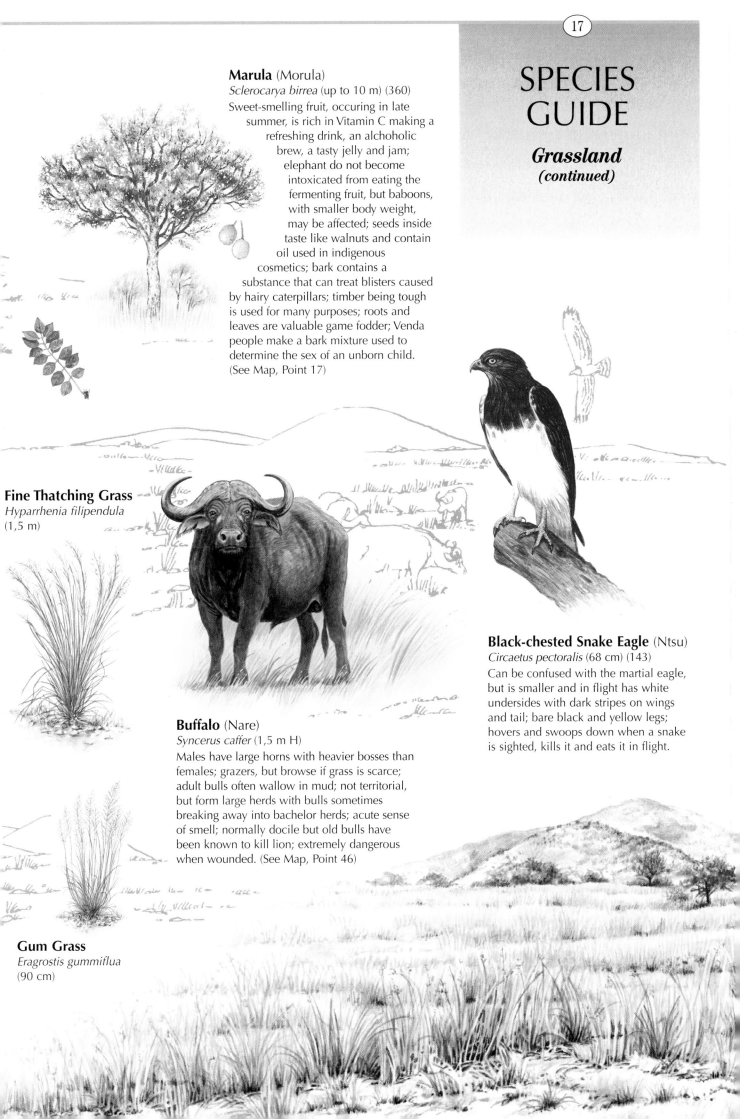

### Marula (Morula)
*Sclerocarya birrea* (up to 10 m) (360)
Sweet-smelling fruit, occuring in late summer, is rich in Vitamin C making a refreshing drink, an alchoholic brew, a tasty jelly and jam; elephant do not become intoxicated from eating the fermenting fruit, but baboons, with smaller body weight, may be affected; seeds inside taste like walnuts and contain oil used in indigenous cosmetics; bark contains a substance that can treat blisters caused by hairy caterpillars; timber being tough is used for many purposes; roots and leaves are valuable game fodder; Venda people make a bark mixture used to determine the sex of an unborn child. (See Map, Point 17)

### Fine Thatching Grass
*Hyparrhenia filipendula*
(1,5 m)

### Black-chested Snake Eagle (Ntsu)
*Circaetus pectoralis* (68 cm) (143)
Can be confused with the martial eagle, but is smaller and in flight has white undersides with dark stripes on wings and tail; bare black and yellow legs; hovers and swoops down when a snake is sighted, kills it and eats it in flight.

### Buffalo (Nare)
*Syncerus caffer* (1,5 m H)
Males have large horns with heavier bosses than females; grazers, but browse if grass is scarce; adult bulls often wallow in mud; not territorial, but form large herds with bulls sometimes breaking away into bachelor herds; acute sense of smell; normally docile but old bulls have been known to kill lion; extremely dangerous when wounded. (See Map, Point 46)

### Gum Grass
*Eragrostis gummiflua*
(90 cm)

## Thickets

### African Olive (Wild Olive) (Motlhare)
*Olea europaea/africana* (up to 7 m) (617)
Common, widespread tree; smooth, shiny dark-green leaves; purple-black, bitter fruits are eaten by animals; wood was used for ornaments. (See Map, Point 61)

### Jacket-plum/Indaba Tree (Mopepenwe)
*Pappea capensis* (up to 10 m) (433)
Hardy, evergreen tree with rough, leathery leaves; soft, hairy berries which split like a jacket to reveal a soft red seed capsule; fleshy part is browsed; used to make jelly and alcoholic beverage; Cecil John Rhodes and Matabele chief Lobengula, met under one of these trees, hence 'Indaba tree'.

### Common Duiker (Phuti/Photi)
*Sylvicapra grimmia* (52 cm H)
Solitary browsers showing preference for tips of plants; rarely drink water; most active at night or cooler parts of day; rely on keen senses of smell and vision; freeze in danger, flee in ducking, zig-zag manner.

(M)

### Tree Squirrel (Setlhora)
*Paraxerus cepapi* (35 cm L, including tail)
Nest in old barbet or woodpecker nests; feed on ground during the day; female produces 2 young, which remain in tree-hole until able to climb up and down; eat fruit, nuts and sometimes insects; enemies are birds of prey, genets and pythons; when meeting a snake they mob it hysterically.

### Vervet Monkey (Kgabo)
*Cercopithecus aethiops* (114 cm L)
Sociable animals which groom each other to remove pests and strengthen bonds; adult male has blue scrotum; prefer fruit and pods, but also eat insects, eggs and small birds; main enemies are leopards and eagles.

(F)

### Steenbok (Phudufudu)
*Raphicerus campestris* (52 cm H)
Solitary or in pairs in established territories; depend on water; when threatened, flee in a zig-zag run, then stop to glance back; young hidden for a few weeks; lie motionless when approached; martial eagles prey on the young.

(F)

(M)

(F)

### Tropical Tent Spider (Segokgo)
*Cyrtophora* species (8 - 20 mm)

### Golden Brown Baboon Spider (Tshere)
*Pterinochilus* species (60 mm)

### Guinea Grass
*Panicum maximum* (2,5 m)

### Spotted Bush Snake (Legwere)
*Philothamnus semivariegatus* (70 - 100 cm; max 126 cm)

## Buffalo-thorn Jujube (Mokgalo)
*Ziziphus mucronata*
(up to 9 m) (447)

Shrub or tree with shiny, fresh-green leaves; paired thorns, one straight, one strongly curved; deciduous, but a few leaves remain in winter; heavily browsed; monkeys, baboons and eland eat the berry-like fruit; local people believe in the magical ability to deflect lightning, and ward off evil spirits; a sacred tree to the Zulus; has many medicinal uses.

# SPECIES GUIDE
## *Thickets*

For thousands of years specific animals have adapted perfectly to this habitat. It is suited to browsers, who have learned to use camouflage and secrecy, for protection. Carnivores, like the smaller cats, hunt here. They rely on surprise attacks, rather than the fast chases of the lioness and cheetah.

Taller trees grow in riverine areas, kloofs and gullies, where water and soil collect. This provides perfect nesting sites for birds, and offers the safety and food required for animals in the breeding season… …watch carefully for the Black R hino and smaller shy antelope, but especially for the many different birds that inhabit these areas.

## Black Rhinoceros
(Tshukudu e Ntsho)
*Diceros bicornis* (1,6 m H)
Endangered species; smaller than White Rhino with hooked, triangular upper lip adapted for browsing; bite off thick, woody sticks; tolerate thorns and natural chemicals of poisonous plants; solitary and unpredictable with nervous energy and curiosity; babies run behind mothers and therefore fall prey to lion; horns consist of compressed hair, sought after in the East as an aphrodisiac and for dagger handles.

## Impala (Phala)
*Aepyceros melampus* (90 cm H)
Dominant males establish territories and spend rutting season chasing females, grunting and snorting; in breeding season one male dominates breeding herd of females, weaker males group as bachelors; out of season females in nursery herds in loose association with bachelor herds; browse and graze on a wide variety of plants; can jump 3 m high and 12 m in length.

**(M)**

## Bushbuck
(Serolobotlhoko)
*Tragelaphus scriptus* (80 cm H)
Found in thickets near water; males are dark brown, females chestnut; shy and mainly nocturnal; solitary animals or in pairs that browse and graze, picking up fruit and flowers dropped by monkeys and other tree-dwellers; strong swimmers; move to shallow water if threatened; main enemy is the leopard.

**(M)**

## Kraal Spike-thorn
*Maytenus polycantha*
(up to 2 m) (401.2)
Shrub-forming impenetrable thickets used to surround kraals; leaves are small, shiny and grow in clusters; reddish fruit capsules contain yellow seeds.

## Thickets

### Doves (Maeba)
Family Columbidae
Predominantly grey with small heads and stout bodies; fly extremely well but spend much time on the ground picking up seeds which are stored in well developed crops; song is typical coo-ing sound.

### Hornbills (Dikorwe)
Family Bucerotidae
Nest in holes in tree trunks, with the female sealed inside with only a slit for the male to pass food through; after 20 days, female breaks out, the chicks reseal the nest and are fed by both parents; ungainly looping flight.

#### Rock Pigeon (Leebarope)
*Columba guinea* (33 cm) (349)
Nest on cliffs; fly in flocks covering great distances to find food.

#### Emerald-spotted Wood-Dove (Greenspotted Dove)
(Leeba) *Turtur chalcospilos* (20 cm) (358)

#### Red-billed Hornbill (Korwe)
*Tockus erythrorhynchus* (46 cm) (458)

#### Cape Turtle Dove (Leeba)
*Streptopelia capicola* (28 cm) (354)

#### Laughing Dove (Tsokwane)
*Streptopelia senegalensis* (25 cm) (355)

#### Black-collared Barbet (Kokopa)
*Lybius torquatus* (20 cm) (464)
Sexes alike; usually in pairs but also in larger groups making raucous noise; eat fruit and insects; also found in riverine areas.

#### Southern Yellow-billed Hornbill
(Korwe) *Tockus leucomelas* (55 cm) (459)

#### Forest Num-num (Morokolo)
*Carissa bispinosa* (up to 2 m) (640.2)
Small, evergreen shrub with green, new stems and Y-shaped (twice-forked) thorns; leaves are shiny and sharp-tipped; edible, delicious, red berries.

#### Cape Glossy Starling (Legodi)
*Lamprotornis nitens* (24 cm) (764)
Small flocks; pair off in breeding season; distinctive 'turr treau' call; feed on insects, fruit and aloe nectar; fond of camp titbits.

#### Arrow-marked Babbler (Letsheganoga)
*Turdoides jardineii* (24 cm) (560)
Move around from tree to tree in noisy groups of about 10; feed mainly on insects, also spiders, small reptiles and fruit; about 7 birds help to build nest.

#### Helmeted Guineafowl (Kgaka)
*Numida meleagris* (58 cm) (203)
Roost in trees at night; congregate in large flocks on the ground where they forage for seeds, bulbs and insects; have been seen removing ticks from warthogs.

#### White-browed Scrub-Robin
*Erythropygia leucophrys* (15 cm) (613)
Usually seen singly or in pairs on ground or in scattered scrub; make varied, clear calls from tree-tops; 2 - 3 eggs laid on ground Oct – Dec.

#### Red Toad
(Segwagwa) *Bufo carens* (7 cm L)
Abundant towards end of summer; travel far in search of a dark, quiet place to spend the winter – shoes left in cupboards often serve this purpose well!

## Giraffe (Thutlwa)
*Giraffa camelopardalis* (3,3m)
Tallest mammal; weighs up to
2 000 kg; browse over 100 tree
species, especially thorn-trees;
not dependant on daily water;
non-territorial, living in
loose social system;
known to eat bones for
extra calcium.

## Bushveld Shepherds-tree (Motlopi)
*Boscia foetida* (up to 5m) (125)
Inner wood and flowers (Aug – Sept) have
rancid smell, hence common name;
edible fruit. (See Map, Point 4)

## Garbage Line Spider
(Segokgo)
*Cyclosa* species
(50 - 150 mm)

## Elephant (Tlou)
*Loxodonta africana* (3,2 - 4m H)
Bulls have rounded foreheads whereas cows' are
angular; have an acute sense of smell and hearing but
limited sight; often a preference for left or right,
shown by one tusk being more worn than the
other; herds are lead by matriarchs; bulls
are solitarily or in bachelor herds; eat
about 300 kg of food, and drink about
160 litres of water a day; although they
damage trees, this helps create low
growth for smaller browsers; visitors
must approach with caution,
especially breeding herds.

## Golden Orb Web Spider
(Segokgo)
*Nephila senegalensis* (25 - 30 mm)

## Tropical House Gecko
(Sepharela-Nkong)
*Hemidactylus mabouia
mabouia* (12 - 15 cm)

# Thickets

**Black-thorn Acacia** (Mongana)
*Acacia mellifera* (up to 8 m) (176)
Tree or shrub forming impenetrable thickets; creamy-white pom-pom flowers in spring; good fire-wood. (See Map, Point 26)

**Puzzle-bush Stamperwood** (Morob
*Ehretia rigida* (up to 4 m) (657)
Common shrub with tangled appearance; clusters of sweetly-scented, lilac flowers Aug – Feb; branches are used in cattle kra as they are believed to subdue bad-tempered oxen; hunters used to believe that pointing these branche at animals will render them weak.

**Cardinal Woodpecker** (Kokopa)
*Dendropicos fuscescens* (15 cm) (486)
Often heard making rapid tapping noises on branches; usually work a tree from bottom up to the top, looking for grubs and insects; excavate holes in dead trees for nesting.

**Green Wood-Hoopoe
(Redbilled Woodhoopoe)**
*Phoeniculus purpureus* (36 cm) (452)
Occur in noisy, restless groups which move from tree to tree, clambering around branches looking for insects, millipedes and small reptiles; they nest in holes made by woodpeckers and barbets.

**Crimson-breasted Shrike**
(Mampa tshibidu)
*Laniarius atrococcineus* (25 cm) (739)
Associated with dry, semi-arid thornveld; vocal birds, seen alone or in pairs, foraging on ground for insects; called 'Reichsvogel' in Namibia as colours are same as German flag.

**African Hoopoe** (Pupupu)
*Upupa epops* (26 cm) (451)
Walks about probing the ground for insects; will sometimes extract insects from the bark of trees; flies in a butterfly fashion; its call is a monotonous *'hoo poop poop'*; smelly nest as they do not remove faeces.

**Common Fiscal Shrike**
(Tlhomedi)
*Lanius collaris* (23 cm) (732
Hunt from perches carrying prey in beaks or feet; sometimes hang prey on thornbushes or fences, returning later to feed, hence the name 'butcher bird'.

**Firefinches**
Family Estrildidae
Gregarious; feed on ground for seed, often at water; host to widow finches, incubating and rearing their young.

**Red-billed Firefinch**
*Lagonosticta senegala* (10 cm) (842)

**Jameson's Firefinch**
*Lagonosticta rhodopareta*
(11 cm) (841)

**Black-headed Oriole**
*Oriolus larvatus* (25 cm) (545)
Utters beautiful, liquid call from tops of tall trees; mainly insectivorous, but will feed on fruit and nectar; it makes a deep well-concealed, moss nest, lined with spider webs and plant material.

**Dark-capped Bulbul
(Black-eyed Bulbul)**
(Rankolokota)
*Pycnonotus barbatus*
(22 cm) (568)
Abundant and common in variety of habitats; gregarious, cheerful, vocal and active; eat insects, fruit and nectar; call sounds like, *'Wake up Gregory'*.

**Fork-tailed Drongo**
(Kuamesi)
*Dicrurus adsimilis*
(25 cm) (541)
Immature birds have white wingpatches, flashed in flight, but adults are totally black; perch at tops of trees; are aggressive, often harassing birds of prey; mimic other birds but main call is a rasping squeak; catch insects in the air, mob other birds, and also eat small birds and sometimes fish.

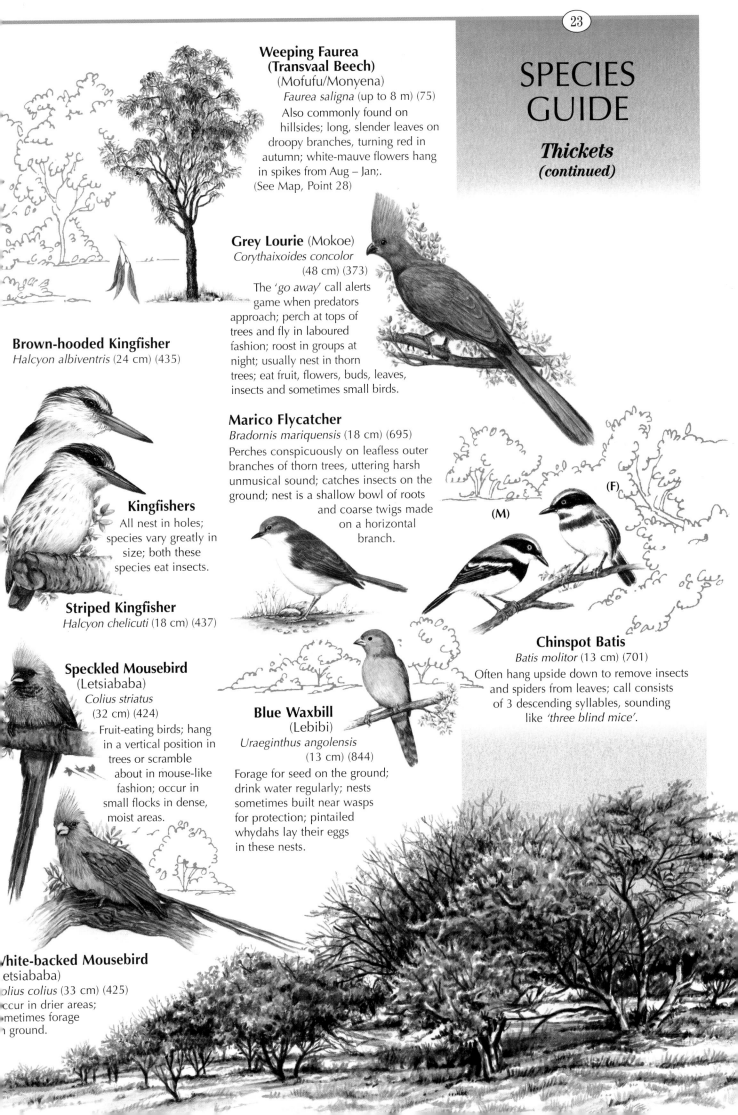

## Weeping Faurea (Transvaal Beech)

(Mofufu/Monyena)

*Faurea saligna* (up to 8 m) (75)

Also commonly found on hillsides; long, slender leaves on droopy branches, turning red in autumn; white-mauve flowers hang in spikes from Aug – Jan;.
(See Map, Point 28)

## Grey Lourie (Mokoe)

*Corythaixoides concolor*
(48 cm) (373)

The '*go away*' call alerts game when predators approach; perch at tops of trees and fly in laboured fashion; roost in groups at night; usually nest in thorn trees; eat fruit, flowers, buds, leaves, insects and sometimes small birds.

## Brown-hooded Kingfisher

*Halcyon albiventris* (24 cm) (435)

### Kingfishers

All nest in holes; species vary greatly in size; both these species eat insects.

## Striped Kingfisher

*Halcyon chelicuti* (18 cm) (437)

## Marico Flycatcher

*Bradornis mariquensis* (18 cm) (695)

Perches conspicuously on leafless outer branches of thorn trees, uttering harsh unmusical sound; catches insects on the ground; nest is a shallow bowl of roots and coarse twigs made on a horizontal branch.

**(M)**     **(F)**

## Chinspot Batis

*Batis molitor* (13 cm) (701)

Often hang upside down to remove insects and spiders from leaves; call consists of 3 descending syllables, sounding like '*three blind mice*'.

## Speckled Mousebird

(Letsiababa)

*Colius striatus*
(32 cm) (424)

Fruit-eating birds; hang in a vertical position in trees or scramble about in mouse-like fashion; occur in small flocks in dense, moist areas.

## Blue Waxbill

(Lebibi)

*Uraeginthus angolensis*
(13 cm) (844)

Forage for seed on the ground; drink water regularly; nests sometimes built near wasps for protection; pintailed whydahs lay their eggs in these nests.

## White-backed Mousebird

(Letsiababa)

*Colius colius* (33 cm) (425)

occur in drier areas; sometimes forage on ground.

# Rocky Areas

## Naboom (Common Tree Euphorbia)

(Ngoge) *Euphorbia ingens* (up to 15 m) (351) Angular, segmented fleshy branches produce a milky latex causing skin irritation and blindness; poison was used by local people to catch fish. (See Map, Point 34)

## Large-leaved Rock Fig (Moumo)

*Ficus soldanella* (up to 7 m) (63)
The white roots split the rocks open; baboons feed on the fallen figs.
(See Map, Point 18)

## Klipspringer (Kololo)

*Oreotragus oreotragus* (60 cm H)
Live in small family groups; mark territory by dung-piles and pheromone secretion from eye-gland; hooves are blunt with long narrow pads to prevent slipping on rocks; coat has course, hollow, flattened hairs which insulate and help to conserve water; rarely drink water; browse on shrubs, fallen leaves, fruit, flowers and pods. (See Map, Point 66)

(F)

(M)

## Klipspringers & Ticks

Certain species of ticks locate scent-marking from eye-gland of klipspringers; wait on twigs for the animal to return to re-scent, then hop on for a bloodmeal!

## Common Cabbage-tree

*Cussonia spicata*
(up to 10 m) (564)
Also found on hillslopes; large leaves are dark bluish-green and digitate (hand-like) with deep fissures; bark is cork-like; wood used by Zulu people in treatment of malaria; leaves provide valuable source of fodder.

## Hard Tick
(Dikgofa)
*Rhipicephalus* species
(3 - 6 mm)

## Bristle-leaved Red Top

*Melinis nerviglumis* (1,2 m)
Leaf sheaths are densely overlapped and hairy with silky pink or white flowering heads; has rolled leaves which help reduce transpiration and conserve water.

## Wall Crab Spider (Flattie)
(Segokgo)
*Selenops* species (15 - 30 mm)
Use lightning speed and camouflage to catch food; keep eggs in white disc-shaped web, woven over small depressions in rock face.

# SPECIES GUIDE
## Rocky Areas

This is the ideal habitat for many different species that have adapted here, because of the safety, food and shelter provided. It is suited to climbing and jumping animals that could not survive in open areas, where speed is needed. Even man was once drawn by these vantage points, from where enemies could be seen, and food easily hunted and gathered.

Rich soil and water collects in crevices and lush vegetation grows. This sets in motion many food chains. Reptiles and dassies bask on rocks, and birds of prey search for them from high above. Baboons come to eat fruit or scorpions, while watching for the leopard. She is lured to caves and secret places to raise her cubs in safety. Perhaps, centuries from now she will still stare across the far valley and in the dead of night, will silently stalk her prey.

### Chacma Baboon (Tshwene)
*Papio ursinus* (1,5 m L)
Largest primate in southern Africa; biggest enemy is the leopard; eats plants, insects, scorpions, fruit, rodents, eggs and even small mammals; highly gregarious, occurring in troops of up to 100 with strict order of dominance; females in season have large crimson backsides and only mate with dominant males; senior males act as sentries and warn other animals of predators.

### Common Russet Grass
*Loudetia simplex* (1,2 m)
Grows in poor, shallow soils in exposed, stony areas and is rarely eaten by animals; flowering heads form attractive golden sprays; often used in thatching and brooms.

### Leopard (Nkwe)
*Panthera pardus* (60 cm H)
Solitary, secretive, nocturnal animals; spend most of the day in hiding; territory is scent-marked with urine; possibly the most dangerous predator when wounded or trapped, using strength, teeth and claws.

### Resurrection Plant (Moswiarula)
*Myrothamnus flabellifolius* (20 - 40 cm)
During winter, this green bush seemingly dies, but miraculously springs to life when given water; has many medicinal uses associated with revitalising the body and treating breast diseases; look out for it on the Nkakane Link. (See Map, Point 22)

### Rock Dassie (Pela)
*Procavia capensis* (54 cm L)
Herbivorous, spending early morning or late afternoon feeding at a furious rate; regularly bask in the sun to increase body temperature; eyesight and hearing acute; very agile with glandular secretions on soles of feet to prevent slipping; it is claimed that they have different alarm calls for eagles, leopards and pythons.

## Rocky Areas

### Lavender Croton
### (Lavender Fever-berry)
### (Moologa)
*Croton gratissimus* (up to 2 m) (328)
Common tree with elongated leaves,
dark-green on top, silver-white dotted
with brown underneath; leaves have a
lavender fragrance which San women
used for perfume.

### Raisin Bush
*Grewia* species (up to 4 m) (460, 462)
Rounded stems; leaves 3 veins from base;
yellow flowers produce edible, lobed fruits
reddish when ripe; wood is used for making
walking sticks and assegai handles.

### Wild-pear Dombeya
### (Common Wild Pear)
(Mokgofa)*Dombeya rotundifolia*
(up to 7 m) (471)
Common tree; rough sand-papery
leaves; clusters of white or pink flowers
appear Jul – Sep; extracts of bark,
roots and leaves used for stomach
ailments and headaches.

### Hard Fern
*Pellaea calomelanos*
Can survive in exposed, hot,
dry places among rocks, by
shrivelling up in dry times
and rehydrating when it
rains; leaves used by local
people to soothe nerves
and treat colds.

### Mother-in-law's Tongue
*Sansevieria* species
Despite its name, is highly prized by
man and animal; used in weaving
and as a painkiller, worm
remedy and
treatment for piles
and varicose veins;
Black Rhino browse in
winter; showy column
of flowers; fruits
Nov – Feb.

### African Rock Python (Tlhware)
*Python sebae natalensis* (3 - 5 m L)
Usually hunts at night, detecting warm-
blooded prey with heat sensors on its lips;
bite is non-venomous, with prey killed by
suffocation e.g. birds, reptiles, small mammals,
including antelope and monkeys; protected species but
vulnerable as skins used in the fashion industry.

### Southern Rock Agama
### (Rankgatakwane)
*Agama atra*
(20 - 25 cm L; max 32 cm)

### Black Mamba (Mokwepa
*Dendroaspis polylepis* (2,5 - 4,2 m L
Common snake; can be found sun-bathing or
rocks, or travelling swiftly through the grass with
coffin-shaped head held high; will readily attack
if threatened; neurotoxic venom causes paralysi
of victim's lungs with death in hours if no
treated with anti-venom; preys on dassies
game-birds, rodents and lizards

### Rock Monitor (Gopane)
*Varanus exanthematicus albigularis*
(0,7 - 1,3 m L)
Huge lizard, related to the Komodo
Dragon; feeds on tortoises, eggs,
insects, small birds, rodents and
carrion; lives in tunnels under rock
overhangs or disused animal burrows or
termite mounds; it is a protected animal.

## SPECIES GUIDE

### Rocky Areas
*(continued)*

**Rock Martin** (Peolwane)
*Hirundo fuligula* (15 cm) (529)
Small brown swallow with square white spotted tail; often flies around with other swallows feeding on insects; perches on rocks; builds neat cup-like nest of mud against vertical cliffs.

**Verreaux's Eagle (Black Eagle)** (Ntsu)
*Aquila verreauxii* (84 cm) (131)
Uncommon, large eagle, totally black, with a white 'V' on the back and rump; yellow feet and cere; live in pairs, forming permanent bonds; nest in winter against sheer cliff faces, utilising the same nest for generations; female lays 2 eggs a few days apart; the older chick kills the younger one; feed mainly on dassies, but also other mammals, terrestrial birds, carrion and rarely reptiles. (See Map, Point 24)

**Mocking Chat**
*Thamnolaea cinnamomeiventris* (22 cm) (593)
Vocal birds with a loud melodious song which mimics about 30 other bird calls; occur in small groups; can be seen running around, sometimes raising tails; drop onto insects on the ground from perch, or jump around in trees in search of fruit.

(F)

(M)

**Red-winged Starling** (Legodi)
*Onychognathus morio* (28 cm) (769)
Slender, elegant, glossy black with chestnut coloured wingtips; often found in large flocks of 100 or more; has a varied diet of fruit, insects, reptiles, ticks and aloe nectar.

**Silky Bushman Grass**
*Stipagrostis uniplumis* (75 cm)
Erect, tufted grass with attractive, feathery 3-awned flowers; grows on sandy soils and in disturbed areas.

**Common Kestrel (Rock Kestrel)**
*Falco tinnunculus* (32 cm) (181)
Can often be seen hovering, then taking prey from the ground; do not build nests, but lay their eggs on ledges, in holes, trees or old nests of other birds; feed on small mammals, lizards, snakes, insects and other birds.

**Robber Fly** (Seboba)
Family Asilidae (24 mm)
Long hairy flies that patrol the rocks actively; large mobile heads with bulging eyes; they grab victims, stab them with the proboscis and suck them dry.

**Lichens**
Can survive extreme conditions very well as are superbly adapted to living on rocks; vulnerable to poisoning by accumulated air pollution; one of oldest plant forms on earth.

## Water Areas

**Karee** (Moshabele)
*Rhus lancea* (up to 7 m) (386)
Spreading, evergreen, frost resistant tree with willow-like appearance; flowers (winter) are yellow-green, in clusters; fruit hangs in tiny grape-like bunches; beer brewed from fermented fruit; tough and durable wood used for fence posts and implement handles.

**River Bushwillow**
**(Modubanoka)**
*Combretum erythrophyllum*
(up to 10 m) (536)
Tall, spreading tree, usually found along riverbanks; fast growing and drought resistant; four-winged papery seeds remain on tree all year in clusters at tips of branches – they are poisonous and if eaten cause hiccupping; browsed by elephant and giraffe.

**Common Reedbuck**
**(Mofele o mohibidu/Motlobo)**
*Redunca arundinum* (90 cm H)
Mothers only suckle babies once a day; baby moves around frequently to avoid predation; prefer tall grass near water and will swim in extreme danger; have sharp alarm whistle, fleeing in rocking-horse motion with tails fanned over backs.

(F)

(M)

**Broad-pod Elephant-root**
**(Sumach Bean)**
(Mosidi/Mositsane)
*Elephantorrhiza burkei* (up to 3 m) (193)
Small deciduous tree or shrub with feathery blue-green *Acacia*-like leaves; large pods can reach 30 cm in length, often splitting and curling in a tight roll; used in the tanning of leather.

**Cape Terrapin** (Rantlapere)
*Pelomedusa subrufa* (28 cm L)

**Foam Nest Frog** (Mololope)
*Chiromantis xerampelina* (7 - 8 cm L)
The foam is sperm that other males have paddled to froth; this holds the eggs before hatching.

**Common Wild Sorghum**
*Sorghum bicolor* (2,5 m )

**Emperor Dragonfly**
**(Seboba)**
*Anax imperator* (7 cm)
Fastest insects in the world; often brightly coloured, especially adult males; territorial predators; they fly over water, scooping up insects in specially adapted legs which form a 'basket'; mating pairs fly in tandem; females dip over water, touching the surface and depositing eggs.

**Striped Stream Frog**
(Segwagwa)
*Rana fasciata* (3,5 cm L)

**Water Monitor**
(Gopane)
*Varanus niloticus*
(1 - 1,4 m L; max 2 m)

# SPECIES GUIDE
## *Water Areas*

Where there is temporary or permanent water, species totally dependent on it, will always be close by. Animals like hippo, waterbuck and the water-birds need water daily. They live here relying on the safety, food and drink provided all year round. Many birds breed near permanent water.

Tiny water organisms play a vital role in a food chain that includes insects, frogs, waders and even crocodiles.

Animals that get enough moisture in the summer from pools, puddles, or plants, come down to dams in the dry winter months. Predators wait… and the peaceful scene is sometimes shattered by the thrill of a kill, or the relief of escape.

### Hippopotamus (Kubu)
*Hippopotamus amphibius* (1,5 m H)

Hippos spend most of the day in water; mate, suckle young and walk underwater creating paths that keep waterways open; sensitive skins protected from ultraviolet rays by a reddish oil secretion; highly territorial, they defend pear-shaped home-ranges; graze at night, often covering up to 10 km while eating up to 130 kg of food; responsible for more human fatalities than any other animal in Africa, moving at speeds of 30 km/h.

### Finger Grass
*Digitaria eriantha*
(1 m)

(M)  (F)

### Common Waterbuck
(Pitlhwa)

*Kobus ellipsiprymnus* (1,3 m H)
Characteristic white ring on rumps; gregarious grazers, browsing occasionally; use water as refuge, sometimes submerging with only nostrils protruding; oily hair aids waterproofing and has a strong turpentine smell.

### Nile Crocodile
(Kwena) *Crocodylus niloticus*
(2,5 - 3,5 m L; max 5,9 m)

Oldest surviving animal on earth; inbuilt barometer detects changes in atmospheric pressure; 50 - 70 eggs laid in hole in sand; eggs on top become males due to greater heat; mother carries young in mouth to water, after which they are independent; prey on antelope, fish and any unsuspecting animal at water's edge; they cannot chew.

## Water Areas

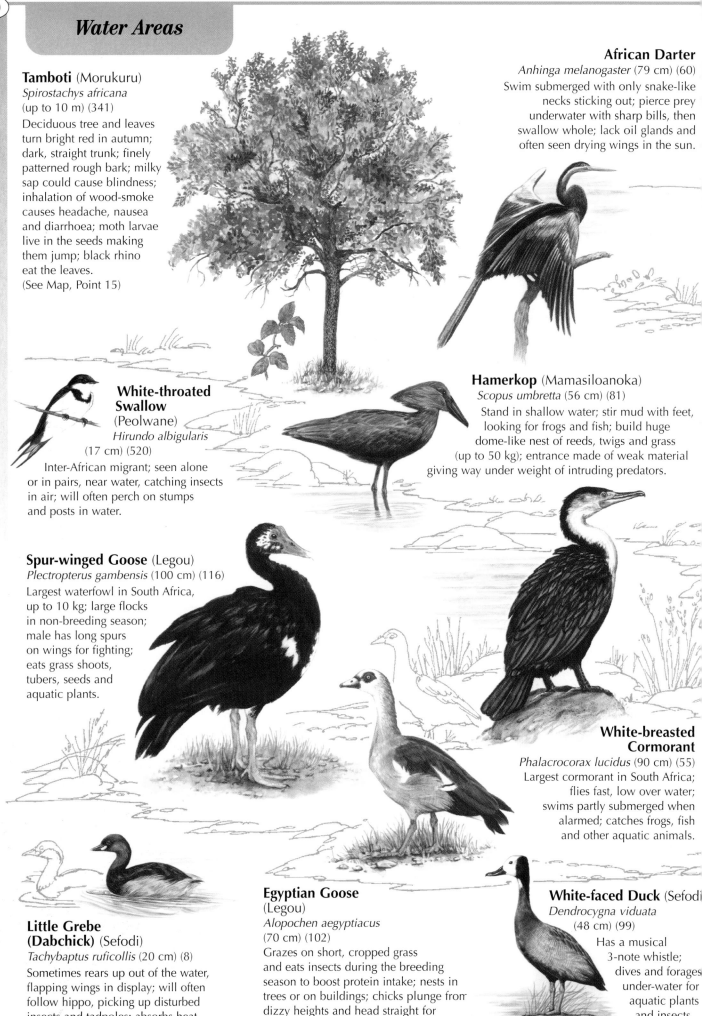

### Tamboti (Morukuru)
*Spirostachys africana*
(up to 10 m) (341)
Deciduous tree and leaves
turn bright red in autumn;
dark, straight trunk; finely
patterned rough bark; milky
sap could cause blindness;
inhalation of wood-smoke
causes headache, nausea
and diarrhoea; moth larvae
live in the seeds making
them jump; black rhino
eat the leaves.
(See Map, Point 15)

### African Darter
*Anhinga melanogaster* (79 cm) (60)
Swim submerged with only snake-like
necks sticking out; pierce prey
underwater with sharp bills, then
swallow whole; lack oil glands and
often seen drying wings in the sun.

### White-throated Swallow
(Peolwane)
*Hirundo albigularis*
(17 cm) (520)
Inter-African migrant; seen alone
or in pairs, near water, catching insects
in air; will often perch on stumps
and posts in water.

### Hamerkop (Mamasiloanoka)
*Scopus umbretta* (56 cm) (81)
Stand in shallow water; stir mud with feet,
looking for frogs and fish; build huge
dome-like nest of reeds, twigs and grass
(up to 50 kg); entrance made of weak material
giving way under weight of intruding predators.

### Spur-winged Goose (Legou)
*Plectropterus gambensis* (100 cm) (116)
Largest waterfowl in South Africa,
up to 10 kg; large flocks
in non-breeding season;
male has long spurs
on wings for fighting;
eats grass shoots,
tubers, seeds and
aquatic plants.

### White-breasted Cormorant
*Phalacrocorax lucidus* (90 cm) (55)
Largest cormorant in South Africa;
flies fast, low over water;
swims partly submerged when
alarmed; catches frogs, fish
and other aquatic animals.

### Little Grebe (Dabchick) (Sefodi)
*Tachybaptus ruficollis* (20 cm) (8)
Sometimes rears up out of the water,
flapping wings in display; will often
follow hippo, picking up disturbed
insects and tadpoles; absorbs heat
in winter by pointing tail to the sun,
exposing the black skin.

### Egyptian Goose
(Legou)
*Alopochen aegyptiacus*
(70 cm) (102)
Grazes on short, cropped grass
and eats insects during the breeding
season to boost protein intake; nests in
trees or on buildings; chicks plunge from
dizzy heights and head straight for
water; females utter a honking sound,
males wheeze; mate for life.

### White-faced Duck (Sefodi
*Dendrocygna viduata*
(48 cm) (99)
Has a musical
3-note whistle;
dives and forages
under-water for
aquatic plants
and insects.

### African Fish Eagle (Kgoadira)
*Haliaeetus vocifer* (73 cm) (148)
Spend most of the day perched in trees watching for fish which they scoop out with their feet, in full flight; loud distinctive call made with head thrown back, even in flight; mate for life. (See Map, Point 27)

### Pied Kingfisher
*Ceryle rudis* (28 cm) (428)
The only black and white kingfisher; hover frequently, with long, straight bills pointing downwards, before splashing into water to catch small fish or insects; nest in holes in sandbanks.

### Hadeda Ibis
*Bostrychia hagedash* (76 cm) (94)
Noisy bird uttering a loud **'haaa'** on take-off and characteristic *'ha ha ha di da'* in flight; small flocks roost in trees and forage on ground, probing their bills deep into the soil for insects; also eat spiders, reptiles, crustaceans, earthworms.

### Three-banded Plover
*Charadrius tricollaris* (18 cm) (249)
Fearless bird, venturing among the feet of elephants and buffalo at water's edge; utters a high-pitched *'wheet'* while running around, suddenly stopping to prod the mud for insects and worms; nest is a mere scraping near the waterline with a few stones added; 1 - 3 well-camouflaged eggs laid.

### Grey Heron
*Ardea cinerea* (1 m) (62)
Plain grey underwing in flight; legs and feet turn reddish in breeding season; usually solitary, stabbing at insects, fish, frogs and crabs; will sometimes feed at night; roost communally.

### Reeds (Motlhaka)
*Phragmites australis* (Up to 3 m)

### Lesser Masked Weaver (Thaga)
*Ploceus intermedius* (15 cm) (815)
Males have black masks in breeding season; weave rounded nests with grass ends sticking out and vertical tunnel-entrance; nests often hang over water; will breed in colonies of not more than 10 birds. (See Map, Point 16)

### Yellow-billed Duck (Sefodi)
*Anas undulata* (60 cm) (104)
Dabbles on water, upending itself to find insects and larvae.

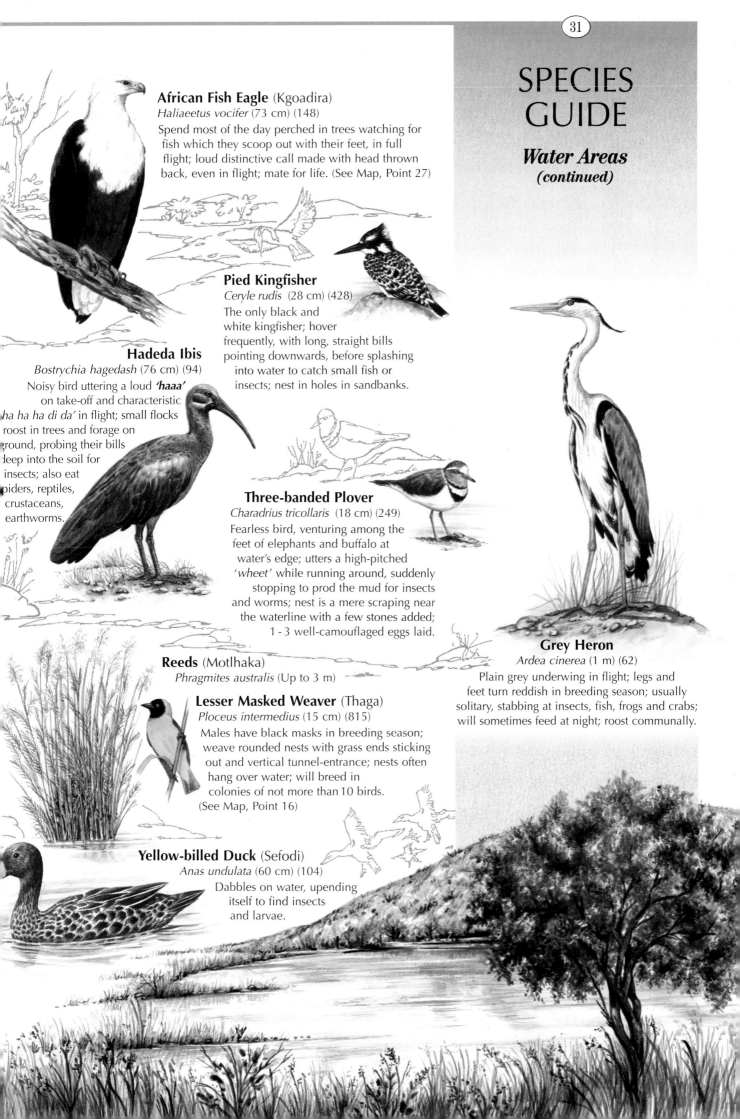

# Sand Roads

## Khaki Weed
*Tagetes minuta* (up to 2 m)
Exotic pioneer plant from South America often found in disturbed areas; strong-smelling, black, rice-like seeds used to make tea; if rubbed on the skin, the oils are believed to keep ticks away.

## Black-jack
*Bidens pilosa*

## Feathered Chloris
*Chloris virgata*
(80 cm)

## Buntings
Family Fringillidae
Small, sparrow-like seed-eaters; forage on the ground.

## Golden-breasted Bunting
*Emberiza flaviventris*
(16 cm) (884)
Sings frequently from a perch, call sounding like *'pretty boy'*.

## Rock Bunting
*Emberiza tahapisi*
(14 cm) (886)
Not as vocal as other buntings, producing a soft *'pee-wee'* call.

## Francolins (Masogo) Family Phasianidae
Chicken-like birds with short tails; different species can be identified by patterns on undersides and by distinctive calls; males have spurs on back of legs; fly fast over short distances with whirring wings.

## Coqui Francolin (Lesogo)
*Peliperdix coqui* (28 cm) (188)

## Crested Francolin
(Lesogo)
*Francolinus sephaena*
(33 cm) (189)

## Natal Francolin (Lesogo)
*Pternistes natalensis*
(38 cm) (196)

## Swainson's Spurfowl (Swainson's Francolin)
(Lesogo)
*Pternistes swainsonii*
(38 cm) (199)

## Leopard Tortoise
(Khudu)
*Geochelone pardalis babcocki*
(30 - 40 cm L; max 72 cm)

## Ants (Ditshoswane)
Family Formicidae
Highly advanced insects; winged male ants die after mating with queen; workers and soldiers are sterile, wingless females; often suck aphids for the sugary sap they secrete, and protect them from other insects in return; Matabele Ants can inflict a painful sting; often seen crossing the road in columns, returning home after raiding a termite mound; each ant will carry up to 5 termites; if the column is disturbed, it emits a high-pitched buzzing noise.

## Puff Adder
(Lebolobolo)
*Bitis arietans arietans*
(60 - 100 cm L)
Exceptionally well camouflaged; slow to move away when threatened, striking with lightning speed when startled or stepped on; potent cytotoxin causes extensive swelling and tissue death – if untreated the victim could lose a limb or die; prey mainly on rodents.

## Dung Beetle
(Khukhwane ya boloko)
Family Scarabaeidae (5 - 50 mm)
Adults and larvae eat dung balls; larvae eaten by genets, civets and baboons.

## Millipede / Songololo (Sebokolodi)
*Doratogonus annulipes* (20 mm)

### Natal Red Top
*Melinis repens*
(1 m)

### Nightshade
*Solanum* species (up to 50 cm)
Belong to the potato family; flowers may be mauve, yellow or white, usually small, star-shaped or circular; common species include bitter apple, poison apple and wild tomato; spherical yellow-red fruits should all be regarded as poisonous.

### Bee-eaters (Merokapula)
Family Meropidae
Feed on insects, especially butterflies, in the air, or they hawk from a perch, usually returning to same perch to eat prey.

### White-fronted Bee-eater
(Morokapula)
*Merops bullockoides*
(23 cm) (443)
Nest colonially in holes along riverbanks.

### Little Bee-eater
(Morokapula)
*Merops pusillus* (17 cm) (444)
Solitary nests in a termite mound or sandbank.

### Warthog (Kolobe ya Naga)
*Phacochoerus aethiopicus* (70 cm H)
Males have prominent tusks and 2 pairs of facial warts to protect eyes during fights; tusks used for digging, defence and fighting; often seen running with tails held stiffly upright; not territorial; feed by kneeling on front legs and dig out roots and rhizomes; sensitive to heat, cold and drought – mud wallowing protects against ultraviolet rays and parasites; use old antbear holes for shelter and breeding.

### Slender Mongoose
(Tshagane)
*Galerella sanguinea*
(60 cm L, including tail)
Solitary, diurnal; will take to trees when threatened; inquisitive, sometimes standing upright before disappearing with flick of tail; omnivorous; young will often follow their mother in procession; main enemy are large birds of prey.

# SPECIES GUIDE
## Sand Roads

Though not a natural habitat, roads attract certain animals, for specific reasons. Some, like reptiles and nightjars, enjoy soaking up the heat that roads give off. The ease of walking with fewer obstacles brings out animals, like tortoises and chameleons, that also enjoy the heat.

Seed-eating birds, like francolins and doves, find food easily in the grasses and in the hedges of bush that grow on the sides of roads. In turn, birds of prey watch eagerly for easy pickings on the open area. Scavengers, owls and many other animals come to eat victims of speeding motorists, especially on main roads. Slow driving will give the visitor rewards. In the open space created by the road, you have the opportunity of seeing many smaller animals normally unseen in the dense bush.

## Large Birds

### Tawny Eagle (Ntsu)
*Aquila rapax* (70 cm) (132)
Not common in this area but present all year round; make large nests at top of trees in winter; seen in pairs or singly; varied, scruffy plumage; recognised by pale-yellow cere and gape ending just below eye.

### Wahlberg's Eagle (Ntsu)
*Aquila wahlbergi* (60 cm) (135)
The only brown eagle to breed in South Africa in summer; also a migrant bird, occuring singly or in pairs; fairly common and recognised by deep yellow cere, gape and legs.

### Vultures (Manong)
Large, scavenging birds of prey; soar high on thermals, using excellent sight to find carcasses; cannot grip prey with talons, but use powerful beaks to tear carcasses open.

### Cape Vulture (Lenong)
*Gyps coprotheres* (1,1 m) (122)
At one time, most common vulture in South Africa, but threatened by farmers as it has been known to attack sheep; nests communally on cliff ledges.

### Lappet-faced Vulture
(Lenong) *Torgos tracheliotus* (1 m) (124)
Largest resident vulture; female larger than male; known to attack live prey.

### White-backed Vulture
(Lenong)
*Gyps africanus* (95 cm) (
Similar to Cape Vul
but smaller; norm
outnumber othe
vultures; lay
egg May –

### Southern Black Korhaan (Black Korhaan)
(Tlatlagwe)
*Eupodotis afra* (53 cm) (239)
Males very noisy, females shy; 1 - 2 eggs laid on ground Oct – Feb.

### Kori Bustard (Kgori)
*Ardeotis kori* (1,3 m) (230)
Heaviest flying bird in the world, with males weighing up to 19 kg; only fly when threatened; usually occur alone, but may congregate in flocks of 30 or more; eat seed, carrion and small vertebrates; male inflates neck and fans tail over back to attract female.

### Red-crested Korhaan
(Tlatlagwe)
*Eupodotis ruficrista* (50 cm) (237)
Very fast fliers; red crest of male seldom seen; males have acrobatic courtship flight.

### Couch Grass
*Cynodon dactylon*
(45 cm)

### Secretarybird
### (Ramolongwana)
*Sagittarius serpentarius* (1,5 m) (118)
Terrestrial bird of prey; loose plume-like quills look like olden day secretaries' pens; walk proudly, stopping to shuffle feet in search of insects, rodents and reptiles; snakes are circled with widespread wings, trampled to death, then swallowed whole.

### Ostrich (Ntshwe)
*Struthio camelus* (2 m) (1)
World's largest bird weighing up to 156 kg; can run up to 70 km/h; eat pebbles to assist digestion; male has a lion-like roar, often at night; male and female protect nest, sometimes giving fatal kicks to intruders.

(M)

**Blue Buffalo Grass**
*Cenchrus ciliaris* (1 m)

# SPECIES GUIDE
## *Large Birds*

Descended from reptiles, birds have survived on earth due to the special adaptation of flight. Although humans have mastered this secret, no man-made machine will ever match the magical flight of birds.

Pilanesberg boasts over 300 bird species. Some are migrants, others permanent inhabitants; some eat carrion or live prey; others eat seeds, fruit or tiny water organisms. And all of them are specifically adpated to their way of life. This page will help identify some of Pilanesberg's larger birds – the "Kings of the Sky", whose flight has inspired people for centuries.

## Experience a Different World

### Death's Head Hawk Moth
(Serurubele)
*Acherontia atropos*
(110 mm)

### Looper Moth
(Serurubele)
*Xylopteryx protearia*

### Pearl-spotted Owl
(Morubitshi)
*Glaucidium perlatum* (18 cm) (398)
Smallest owl in southern Africa
weighing 50 gm; has false eyes
on back of head; active at dawn
and dusk; often mobbed by other
birds when resting; hunts insects, birds
and bats; call is a repetitive ascending
'tee tee tee tee teeu teeu teeu'
then descending.

### Praying Mantis
(Maseletswana)
*Sphodromantis gastrica* (85 mm)

### Common Striped Skink
*Mabuya striata striata*
(18 - 25 cm L)

### Spotted Eagle Owl
(Morubitshi)
*Bubo africanus* (47 cm) (401)
Most common owl in southern Africa; has
slit ears behind the eyes; hunts rodents,
small mammals, reptiles and birds; lays
eggs under rocky overhangs, in hollow
tree-stumps, or in other birds' nests;
call is a typical hooting 'hu hoo'.

### Common Cricket
(Senyetse)
*Gryllus bimaculatus* (28 mm)

### Aardvark / Antbear (Thakadu)
*Orycteropus afer* (160 cm L, including tail)
Strong bear-like claws dig for ants and termites, then uses 30 cm,
sticky tongue; excavated termite mounds become burrows for many
other animals like hyaena, warthog and even bats and
owls; solitary, has very poor eyesight but
keen senses of smell and hearing; has scent
glands between back legs.

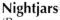

### Nightjars
(Bomamauwane)
Family Caprimulgidae
(23 - 28 cm) (404 - 408)
Well-camouflaged birds
with long, pointed wings; fly silently
as they hawk insects, especially beetles;
roost and nest on the ground moving
their eggs when they suspect detection.

### Large-spotted Genet
(Nakedi/Tshipa)
*Genetta tigrina*
(100 cm L, including tail)
Black-tipped tail distinguishes it
from small-spotted genet; each one has
own unique body pattern; stalk prey in
leopard fashion, catching insects, spiders,
birds, reptiles and small rodents.

### African Civet
(Tsaparangaka)
*Civettictis civetta* (40 cm H)
Claws are doglike and non-retractable;
territorial and solitary; dung contains seed,
hair and exoskeletons of millipedes;
secretion from anal glands was
once used in perfumes.

### Porcupine (Noko)
*Hystrix africaeaustralis* (85 cm L)
Largest rodent in Africa; will walk
backwards towards an intruder
with vibrating quills raised,
sometimes inflicting fatal wounds;
can travel 20 km a night foraging
for tubers, bulbs or roots; ring-barks
trees and gnaws bones to sharpen
incisors and obtain minerals.

### Spotted Dikkop
(Mmutlanakana)
*Burhinus capensis* (44 cm) (297)
Insectivorous; can be seen sleeping
during the day in shade; run with
head low when disturbed; calls
a piping 'ti ti ti ti tee' rising in pitch
and volume, then dying down.

# NIGHT SPECIES

## Experience a Different World

As night falls, stealth, secrecy and surprise spread across the African bush. Now, specialised and unusual species venture out from their daytime hiding, to take advantage of the darkness. Adaptations of sight have made animals like cats, owls, bats and bushbabies, successful nocturnal hunters.

The hunted, who lack this visual advantage, are alert to every sound and every smell. Night animals can also be seen around sunset, before darkness falls. You may also be lucky to spot these nocturnal animals in the early dawn.

### Lesser Bushbaby
(Kgajwanamasigo)
*Galago moholi* (37 cm L, including tail)
Live in trees; forage alone for gum and insects but sleep in family groups in a platform nest with tail and hands covering huge eyes; wipe urine on their feet to scent-mark; make sounds like a baby crying; preyed on by genets and owls.

### Aardwolf (Mmabudu/Mabudu)
*Proteles cristatus* (50 cm H)
Long mane often raised in excitement; long curved canines, other teeth reduced in size; eats up to 200 000 insects a night, mainly termites.

### Brown Hyaena
(Phiri)
*Hyaena brunnea* (80 cm H)
Long mane erected when alarmed, making it look fearsome; scavenger but also hunts small prey, using excellent sense of smell; white droppings characterised by high hair content; territorial males have large home-ranges, marked by scent paste from anal glands. (See Map, Point 43)

### Caracal (Thwane)
*Felis caracal* (45 cm H)
Rare solitary animal; only eats fresh prey; males fiercely defend territories; kittens are helpless at birth and are well hidden.

### Scrub Hare (Mmutla)
*Lepus saxatilis* (55 cm L)
Can often be seen darting ahead of cars at night; a grazer that eats its own dung pellets to obtain full nutrients; males fight viciously over females; unlike rabbits, baby hares can run soon after birth; their defence is to lie still with ears flattened; they also swim well; preyed on by many carnivores and large birds of prey.

# HISTORY

## *Humans and Nature*

Many people say that the Garden of Eden lay in Africa, a natural paradise where people and animals lived side by side. History was born here, and for millions and millions of years, man and animal co-existed, changing and surviving within the protection of the ancient volcano. Today, this is still so, and the story continues to unfold.

### Early Stone Age

2,5 million years ago, our early ancestors invented the first tools – crude hand axes, choppers, irregular cutting flakes, and later, multi-purpose axes and cleavers. This development was as important then, as landing on the moon is to us now.

This period lasted for 2 million years. Early people depended solely on their environment and on their own growing intelligence. They gathered food or scavenged for it, but had not yet learned to hunt large game. Like many of the animals, they were the prey of predators like the sabre-toothed tiger (see illustration showing tiger tooth marks). But unlike other mammals, stone age people ran on two legs and had the use of their hands.

### Middle Stone Age

Between 200 000 and 40 000 years ago a new age began – the spine of prehistoric man had straightened. We call these people Homo Sapiens. They had developed more advanced tools, like sharp stone points and flake blades. To increase their safety and comfort, they took shelter in caves and lit fires against the freezing cold. This period saw the last Ice Age cover the earth in frozen snows and glaciers.

By then, Homo Sapiens had become skilled hunters. The common hunting technique was to drive game into pit traps. There is evidence that by the end of this period a number of animal species had already been hunted into extinction by humans.

**TOOLS AND WEAPONS OF TODAY AND YESTERDAY**

## Late Stone Age

This period occurred between 40 000 BC and 300 AD. It is associated with the San who were hunter-gatherers, and the Khoekhoe who were stock herders of cattle and goats. About 6 000 years ago the climate became much warmer, making survival easier. This was assisted by the development of new tools, like the scraper, and of course the bow and arrow. The San were very skilled hunters. With this new technology, they had time for leisure and time to think. They painted on rocks and made engravings, telling the stories of their lives and their religious beliefs. There are some fine examples of rock art in the Park, but they are well off the beaten track.

## Early Iron Age

In about 300 AD, huge changes swept the sub-continent. Bantu speaking people arrived from the north with new ways and a new technology. This transformed the area forever. They brought crops and the knowledge of iron. They also smelted copper and gold, made pottery and kept domestic stock. A new concept was born – the acquisition of wealth.

For the first time, humans took more than just their basic needs from nature, and this placed significant stress on the environment. Iron smelting needed charcoal and there was plenty of this to be found in the dense woodlands and forests. In addition, bush had to be cleared to make way for crops like cow-peas, sorghum, millet and ground beans. Society revolved around keeping goats and cattle, and villages were built around the animal kraals. To enter the village, visitors would first walk through the kraal to see the wealth and strength of the chief and his people. Basic survival was now softened by the security of wealth.

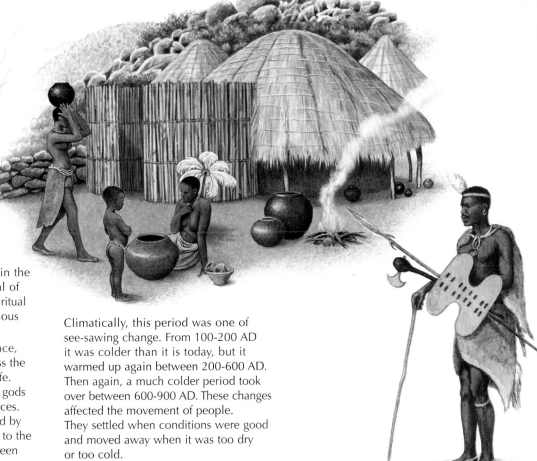

Remains of skeletons and graves in the area show that ochre, symbolical of blood, was used for burials. This ritual was possibly one of the first religious sparks in human history.

The San lived a nomadic existence, following game and rainfall across the vast African plains. Rain meant life. Drought often meant death. Rain gods were invoked through trance dances. Similar rituals were later practiced by Tswana people who built shrines to the rain god. Such shrines have been found in Pilanesberg.

Climatically, this period was one of see-sawing change. From 100-200 AD it was colder than it is today, but it warmed up again between 200-600 AD. Then again, a much colder period took over between 600-900 AD. These changes affected the movement of people. They settled when conditions were good and moved away when it was too dry or too cold.

Despite their greater security, people were still dependent on nature. They moved with the changes of climate and season, and with the movement of game. They still obeyed nature's laws, but they had learned to use it to their advantage.

# HISTORY

## *Humans and Nature*
### *(continued)*

## Late Iron Age

Between 1000 AD and the 1830's, the population in the North West area increased significantly. Inevitable conflict lay ahead. The first half of this millennium was characterised by settlements on foothills of mountains. From about 1600 AD, large stone structures were built on the tops of hills, from where enemies could be seen easily, and the village better defended. Huge 'mega-sites' (1 - 3 kilometres across), housing up to 20 000 people, sprung up on large, open areas in the North West. Such a site can be seen at Malokwane, south-west of the Pilanesberg. Within Pilanesberg however, smaller sites were built on foothills. From here a village had good views, but at the same time, was well hidden from enemies. There were no 'mega-sites' in Pilanesberg. This meant less stress on the environment.

Between 1400 and 1850, climatic changes occurred once again – a cold, dry period (the Little Ice Age) was followed by warmer, wetter conditions. Around 1800, flooding rains and much higher temperatures brought prosperity to the land and people.

With more and more people entering the area that is now the North West, it was not long before competition for resources shattered the peace.

The late 18th and early 19th century was a time of great turbulence and violence. Sometimes known as the Mfecane, or the 'scattering', this time saw many chiefdoms and people move around within South Africa. New chiefdoms moved into the North West area.

## The Bakgatla

Between 1700 and 1750, the Bakgatla people established themselves near present-day Saulspoort (at the northern tip of the Park). They belonged to the Tswana linguistic group. Under the leadership of Chief Masselane, they trekked from Hammanskraal, near present day Pretoria. But the new pastures were ruled by the Batlhako tribe, and for a while the Bakgatla had to pay tribute to live there. When they refused to continue payment, war broke out. The Bakgatla won and enjoyed some years of dominance in the area.

Pilanesberg is named after the Bakgatla chief, Pilane, who ruled between 1825 and 1850.

No one could have risen to power at a more difficult time, because in 1825, the Ndebele warlord, Mzilikaze, swept into the region. He brought turbulence and terror, subduing Pilane's people, imposing taxes and forcing them to look after his cattle. Mzilikaze's war parties caused havoc throughout the North West. With so many corpses littering the bushveld, lions developed a taste for human flesh. People built their huts on platforms or in trees to be safe from these marauding lions.

**PILANESBERG'S
HISTORICAL
TIME-LINE
1 mm = 2 000 years**

EARLY STONE AGE 2 500 000 - 200 000 BC

By the end of the 1800's, European settlers had established themselves permanently and had assumed control in the region. Indigenous people could not dispute the power of guns and horses and were quickly subdued.

Then a new force, the army of the British Empire, arrived to challenge the power of the Boers. Although the second Boer War (1899-1902), did not directly affect the Pilanesberg, the whole region was influenced economically, politically and environmentally.

Europeans continued to rule the land for almost another century.

## Arrival of Settlers from Europe

Around this time missionaries and European settlers began to move into the area. Mzilikaze did not tolerate their presence, except for one extraordinary case. To this day, it remains a fascinating story – the missionary, Robert Moffat entered the region in 1829. He and the Ndebele warlord struck up an instant friendship. Other trespassers were violently chased out but Mzilikaze regarded Moffat as a friend, and even a brother.

Mzilikaze's reign of terror lasted until a combined force of Tswana, Griqua and European settlers drove him out. This was not the first, or last time, that black and white settlers joined to oust a common enemy. The Ndebele fled to southern Zimbabwe and established themselves in Bulawayo.

In 1863 the Dutch Reformed Church established a mission station at Saulspoort. The Bakgatla chief, Kgamanyane, Pilane's son, converted to Christianity. Even today, most Bakgatla are still members of the church. However they have retained many of the old traditions, and still have the same totem animal, the vervet monkey. They also still practice the old Tswana initiation rites. Known as *bogwera*, this teaches the laws and marriage customs of the people as well as knowledge of the environment. It usually takes place in winter and can last 2 - 3 weeks. Young men must bathe in a cold stream and undergo circumcision, before entering adulthood.

## Further Influences

Over this last century, cycles of conflict and resolution, and the rapid advance in technology, have left their mark on the Pilanesberg. The most dramatic effect on the environment came from mechanised agriculture, large herds of domestic stock, and huge hunting expeditions. This saw the gradual disappearance of wild animals, and the temporary destruction of natural habitats.

Smaller influences on the environment had always occurred. For instance Iron Age communities planted *Euphorbia* trees around their homes. These were regarded as magical and medicinal trees, and can still be seen at old village sites in the Park.

A direct influence of nature on man came from the surface water in Pilanesberg. Volcanic rock formations here contain large amounts of fluoride. This is taken up in the water and causes the teeth of long-term inhabitants in the area to go brown (dental fluorosis). At one time, it was said that they could not believe the pure white teeth of newcomers to the area. Today water is piped in from other sources.

The most dramatic influence that man and nature have had on each other in the Pilanesberg, happened very recently. For the first time in the area, people came to assist nature, and not only use it for their own benefit.

**In 1979 the Pilanesberg Park was born...**

PRESENT DAY
LATE IRON AGE 1000 AD - 1830
EARLY IRON AGE 300 - 1000 AD

LATE STONE AGE 40 000 BC - 300 AD

MIDDLE STONE AGE 200 000 - 40 000 BC

# PILANESBERG PARK

## *Creation and Conservation*

Creating the Pilanesberg Park has been a long and complicated process. Since its birth in 1979, dedicated people have nurtured and nourished it. Today it still requires huge effort, careful planning and a vision of the future.

By the year 2 000 AD, some 80 million eco-tourists, worldwide, will visit places like Pilanesberg every year. As more and more of us enjoy the outdoors, we have to ask – can nature sustain itself, as well as us? And how can we give it a helping hand?

These pages show that Pilanesberg is a managed system, involving veld, animal and people management. This is the way to ensure future generations will also benefit from our natural heritage.

## Park History

Pilanesberg Park was first conceived in 1969. It took ten years of research and legislation before it finally opened on 8 December 1979. But before it could be stocked with game, the 55 000 hectare area had to be prepared.

The first step was to remove all evidence of mechanised farming and mining. Houses, fences, windmills, pumps and mining equipment were dismantled and trucked away. Tons of alien vegetation were removed and indigenous vegetation was seeded in its place. The battle to reclaim eroded land began. Eventually, the area was fenced and Operation Genesis began.

Generously funded by the South African Nature Foundation, and many other organisations, this operation remains the largest game translocation in the world. 5 957 animals of 19 different species were initially moved in from parks across southern Africa. Even the fabled Noah did not have to contend with 50 elephants, 1937 impala, or 19 critically endangered Black Rhino, to mention a few. Due to veterinary restrictions, most animals were quarantined in a 1 200 hectare boma, before final release.

Translocating animals to and from Pilanesberg continues. So does the management of these animals and the habitats in which they live.

In addition, management must take care of approximately 120 000 visitors a year...

## Veld Management

Conserving habitat is of vital importance. Without their habitats, no animals would survive. A few aspects of veld management are outlined here.

- Erosion is controlled by building rock packs, gabions, contour drains, dams and weirs. This prevents valuable soil being washed away.
- Most of Pilanesberg is covered in unpalatable sourveld. Veld burning is necessary as it encourages palatable grass to grow.
- Alien plants which are poisonous to game and destructive to natural habitats, are always being removed.
- Good veld management is the basis of good animal management.

## People Management

Large numbers of visitors could have a negative impact on the Park. But revenue from tourism also keeps the Park alive. A delicate balance is therefore needed between people and the Pilanesberg. Looking after visitors includes the building and maintainance of roads, hides, picnic and view sites. This is an ongoing task aimed at making your visit more enjoyable.

Law enforcement is very important. Respecting the Park's laws allows management to get on with looking after the animals and their habitats.

## Animal Management

Today it is said that animals must 'pay their way' if they are to survive in such a full and competitive world. Wildlife must benefit people, and people must benefit wildlife. Here are a few points that help to ensure this:

- Excess game is translocated to other parks. In 1994, Pilanesberg sold 19 white rhino for R361 000. This money benefits the Park and the people living around it.
- A game census is conducted every year. If there are too many animals, some must be culled. This prevents the destruction of habitats.
- Veterinary control prevents disease. Constant research and monitoring of animals helps keep a sustainable natural balance in the Park.
- Scout patrols guard against poachers and check that fences are intact.

Looking after our natural heritage is a 24 hour a day job for the Park's management team. But it is important to realise that by being here, and obeying the laws, you too are making a positive difference.

**Thank you for keeping Pilanesberg beautiful.**

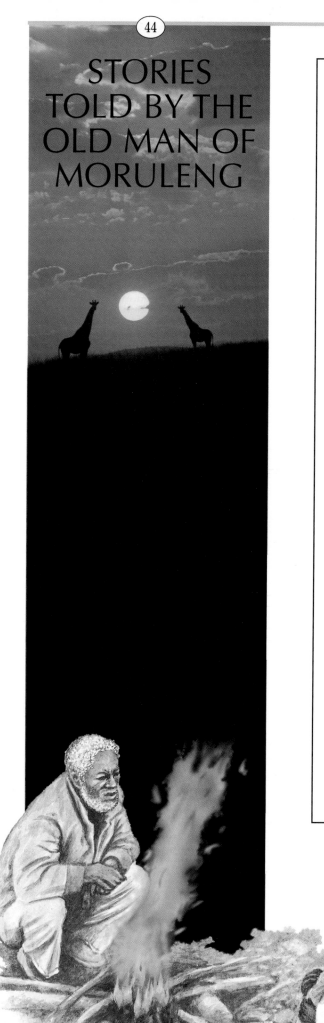

# STORIES TOLD BY THE OLD MAN OF MORULENG

Pilanesberg is a unique area where,
after massive volcanic upheavals,
a natural sanctuary was created within rings of mountains.
For thousands of years animals, man and plants have lived
here relying on one another, or fighting each other, for
food, shelter and homes for their young.

Discovering Pilanesberg can be more than just
a glimpse of one, two or (if you are lucky),
three of the Big Five.

The following pages are designed to help you enjoy
your visit to the maximum, and to give you an
understanding of the rules of the Park.

The rules are there to keep you safe
– the Big Five are not given that name lightly!
There are also rules to keep Pilanesberg as beautiful,
peaceful and unspoilt as it is now.

**Stories told by
the Old Man of Moruleng**
(Pages 45-47)

These stories highlight cultural information from
the Bakgatla and Bakubung people.
(See pages 40 and 45-47.)

**Pilanesberg Map**
(Pages 48-49)

This Map will help you plan your trip,
and guide you as you travel.
It also gives you distances, a summary of facilities,
and the numbers for the Points of Discovery.

**Points of Discovery**
(Pages 50-57)

From the fascinating world of insects, to magical and
medicinal trees, these Discovery Points will provide
the clues as to where… and why…
and how it all happens in Pilanesberg.

THE OLD MAN OF MORULENG

One day I was sitting at **Moruleng, the Place of the Marulas,** eating the juicy fruits, when an Old, Old Man came to me. He sat down. He did not speak for a very long time but sat quietly, listening, and watching the bush. Much later, by the fire, he began to speak, and his voice glowed like the setting sun.

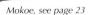

**"You**, know, it is good to enjoy the peace and quiet of this place. When I was a boy I learned many secrets from the bush because I was always quiet and patient. Not like **Mokoe the Grey Lourie** whose noisy call says *'go away'*. Some local people believe that even if you imitate the call of Makoe, your lips will dry up and crack?" With this the Old Man smiled.

*Mokoe, see page 23*

**"You know"**, the Old Man said, "I myself remember the stories my grandfather told. He, like me, was of the **Bakgatla Tribe, the People of the Monkey.** It is our totem animal, and it is honoured and respected by the people of the Pilanesberg. We believe, to eat the flesh of the monkey will make the gods very angry and they will blow the roof off your house."

*Kgabo, see page 18*

*Nare, see page 17*

**"The Bakubung Tribe, the People of the Hippo,** believe the same of the hippo. It is their totem. Long ago people believed this was the truth. Today it is more like a story for most of us, but it is an important part of our culture. ***And we still respect all animals, and all cultures.***"

**"It** can be dangerous, especially if **Tlou the Elephant, Tau the Lion, Tshukudu the Rhino and Nare the Buffalo** are around. In Setswana we say *'e re o gopola tshukudu o ikanye sethlare'*, meaning if you even think of a rhino, you must hide away. In English we say *'speak of the Devil and he will appear'*."

**"There** are many wonderful stories in the bush", he continued. "They have been told to each generation for thousands and thousands of years. Some of it is wisdom, some of it may just be stories … Do you know old Rapula? Well, he had problems with his wife and they could not have children, so the Traditional Healer told him to eat the bark of **Morokolo the Num-num Tree.** Well, after that, they had many, many children." Again, the Old Man smiled, his eyes twinkling with humour and wisdom."Yes, the bush has great magic, but if you destroy it, disturb, or spoil it, you will never see the magic or the power, or the beauty of nature."

*Morokolo, see page 20*

*Tau, see page 15*

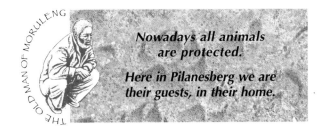

*Nowadays all animals are protected.*

*Here in Pilanesberg we are their guests, in their home.*

**"Now Nkwe the Leopard** is a difficult animal to see and photograph. But we often see his tracks all over the Park, especially at **Mankwe, the Place of the Leopard.** You know that it is a sacred animal for our people. Killing a leopard was a crime punishable by death. The only one allowed to wear the skin was **Kgosi the Chief**."

## Stories told by the old man

It is important not to feed any of the animals or birds. They all know how to feed themselves best.

"**I**f you go fast you won't see much game. The animals' camouflage will deceive your eyes. And by driving off-road you might destroy someone's home, or drive over their young. Small creatures, like children, are all important in the chain of life."

*Korwe, see page 20*

"**T**alking of children, some people used to call my father **Korwe, the Hornbill**, because he was like this bird, who will go hungry as long as his chicks are well fed. Animals, like humans, protect their young."

"**N**ow here is an interesting story about **Tshukudu the Rhino** and children. Did you know the white rhino calf always walks in front of the mother? We say '*Tshukudu kwa gobe e isiwa ke ngwana.*' This means '*that children always lead their parents into trouble.*'" With this the Old Man burst into laughter.

"**H**ere is another story about children and **Legodi the Glossy Starling**. It is said that if a spoilt child wants this bird, you must give it to him, because the bird will peck the child and teach it a lesson."

*Legodi, see page 20*

"**Y**ou know to learn nature's many secrets we must just watch and try to change it as little as possible. We have threatened so many animals already. This is why we do not feed the animals. By doing so we create dependency. After a while animals cannot feed themselves, they starve, or have to be shot by rangers – especially **Tshwene the Baboon**."

Throughout the book Setswana names of the species have been added where possible.

*Tshwene, see page 25*

"**O**ne animal that most people believe is very dangerous is **Noga the Snake**. But snakes are good. They control pests like rodents. Local people say if you see Noga, you must stand with one foot on top of the other to keep yourself from running away. If you are dead still, snakes will leave you alone.

**But it is always best to be careful when walking.**"

"**A**nother reptile is **Gopane the Monitor Lizard**. It is believed that if you kill it, it will bring on a storm, but if you turn it around, it will stop the wind. An old story goes that this lizard sucks milk from the goat by winding its tail around the goat's legs and then milking it until it actually starts to bleed.

**Can you imagine?**
**It is good to imagine!**"

*Pitse e Tilodi, see page 13 & Thutlwa, see page 21*

*Gopane, see page 26*

"**M**yth, magic and healing are all part of our local culture. Many people laugh, but today they are learning to see the value in the old stories and to use plants more and more. Plants are great healers you know. We talked of magic before – now many trees have magical powers too, and many myths surround them."

"**O**ld people with great wisdom believe that to cut **Morula the Marula Tree** in winter, will bring on storms. We use the tree to help cure colds, diarrhoea, dysentery and to make delicious jelly and beer. The marula is like a natural restaurant for man and animals in Africa."

"**M**osetlha the Weeping-wattle is also said to have magical powers. If one of a couple dies, the survivor must drink wattle bark to cleanse the blood of the dead person. If both people die, we say *'Baile – they are gone'*."

*Morula, see page 17*

*Mosetlha, see page 14*

"**Z**ulu people say the thorns of **Mokgalo the Buffalo-thorn** will wipe out a dead person's spirit and bury it. It is believed that Mokgalo is home to their ancestors. And the tree is used as a pain killer; also to treat infections, dysentery, lumbago and chest complaints; and as a protection against lightning."

***Trees are great healers and we must look after them.***

"**U**nmanaged fires destroy these important plants. Today, because of fences, animals cannot escape if there is a fire. Do you know there is a bird that is said to bring fire? Some say that if **Letlekere the Lilac-breasted Roller** perches on your tree or house, it brings bad luck and 'invites' lightning and fire."

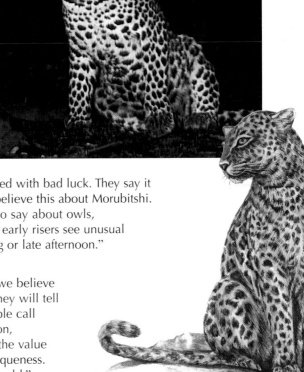

"**M**orubitshi the Owl is another bird traditionally associated with bad luck. They say it can 'invite' witches to your house. Many cultures all over the world believe this about Morubitshi. But owls are really good as they eat rodents and other pests. We also say about owls, *'Morubitshi ga o bonwe, o bonwe ke Motsoga pele'*, which means only early risers see unusual things. And the best time for discovery in Pilanesberg is early morning or late afternoon."

"**N**ow **Pupupu the African Hoopoe** we believe brings good luck. Look for these birds! Maybe they will tell you something in your dreams. What some people call superstition, other people may call belief, religion, psychology or culture. It is important to realize the value of culture. Culture gives people identity and uniqueness. And African culture is one of the oldest in the world."

***We are happy to share this great richness with you.***

*Nkwe, see page 14*

"**I**t is no laughing matter to run out of water, or to be stuck in the bush overnight. I know. Once when Pilanesberg was still farmland, I followed a lost cow way past **Dithabaneng, the Place of the Small Hills**, and I got lost. That night I heard **Nkwe the Leopard** coughing. I did not sleep much in that uncomfortable tree! And the next day I was so thirsty. Luckily…"

By now it was dark and the Old Man continued to tell stories about our animals long into the night. He spoke about them as if they were his friends and I know that, yes, they were his friends.

# PILANESBERG MAP

Elephant, see page 21

**Setswana and English**

On pages 45-47 are the stories of the Old Man of Moruleng where many Setswana names are translated into English. Below are other Setswana names used on the Pilanesberg Map.

**Kgabo** – Monkey
**Kololo** – Klipspringer
**Kwalata** – Sable Antelope
**Ntshwe** – Ostrich
**Thutlwa** – Giraffe
**Tshepe** – Springbok

**Kgama** – Red Hartebeest
**Kukama** – Gemsbok
**Lenong** – Vulture
**Phiri** – Hyaena
**Tilodi** – Zebra

Tlhatlhatganyane

Maologane

## PARK GATES OPEN

NOV – FEB: 05:30 – 19:00
MAR – APR: 06:00 – 18:30
MAY – AUG: 06:30 – 18:00
SEP – OCT: 06:00 – 18:30

## DISTANCES AND TRAVEL TIMES

- Manyane to Pilanesberg Centre – **11 km : 33 mins**
- Bakgatla to Pilanesberg Centre – **8 km : 24 mins**
- Kwa Maritane to Manyane – **23 km : 1 hr 9 mins**
- Bakubang to Pilanesberg Centre – **15 km : 45 mins**
- Pilanesberg Centre round trip – **40 km : 2 hrs**
  (along Moloto/Sefara and Tlou)

Matlhorwe

Moloto

Moloto

58 P V
57

18.3

59

P

61

Batlhako Dam

Marutlhware

Ratshwane

Sefara

Nare

Lenong View

47 28
22 28 44

52

Tlou

1.5 Tlou Dams

Makor Dam

Tshukudu eNtsho

Moloto

Tlou Link 1.5

Tlou

62
0.2
0.3

1.3

Ruighoek Dam
46
45
H V

Kukama

1.0

5.6

Nare

2.0

Ntshwe 3.7

46

3.3

Ntshwe

2.8

Tshukudu Lodge
42

Kgama 1.8

Kgama 5.4

41

1.0

P

H

Lengau Dam

Kubu Dam
Kubu

39

3.7

Kubu 2.5

Bopitikwe

Bakubung Lodge
37
1.9

Bakubung Gate

4.1

Ledig

1   0                                              6 km

N

4.4

# Pilanesberg Map

Thabazimbi

Saulspoort

9.4

3.0

6.7

2.9

4.9

Bakgatla Gate

Bakgatla Complex

10

Moruleng

9

4.0

Ratlhogo Waterhole

11

1.1

Korwe 1.8

1.5

1.0

12

1.4

Kgabo

Dithabaneng Dam

Dithabaneng 3.4

8

Malatse Dam

7

Phiri Loop

1.1

1.8

Dithabaneng 4.8

8.0

Thutlwa 3.2

56

55

0.4

Tau 4.5

2.3

Korwe 4.8

Korwe

Dithabaneng

5

Mothata Scavenger Hide

4

3

0.9

51

Tlou 1.7

60

13

Bakenkop

65

Mothata Picnic Site

Potokwane

3.0

0.7

1.3

Manyane

2

Pilanesberg Centre

50

0.2

Tshwene 0.6

0.8

0.3

Tshwene

1.1

0.7

0.9

Tshwene 1.5

6

0.8

0.6

Tilodi Dam

1.0

0.3

1.1

1

Complex

0.6

0.5 0.6

Hippo Loop

32

Thiwe

2.5

1.2

33

17

1.5

14

Nkwe

0.4

16

15

Tilodi 2.8

Manyane Gate

6.3

Ⓥ

Mankwe Dam

31

Ⓗ

0.3

36

P

35

Fish Eagle

34

1.4

27

Motlobo

1.4

27

Mankwe

1.2

Ⓥ

Twin Dams

18

19

Mogwasi

Kubu 2.4

Letsha 4.0

28

26

Kwalata 2.5

25

Tshepe 2.8

Thabavadiotso

20

Nkakane 5.6

21

Ⓥ

Nkakane

0.5

29 30

6.0

Mankwe

23

Tshepe 3.0

21

13.0

oga 3.0

Ⓥ

Magare

Maritane

24

Tshepe 9.8

67 66

65

Masibudule

Lost City

Kwa Maritane Lodge

63

64

1.3

n City

4.0

Kwa Maritane Gate

R565

3.3

1.7

Pilanesberg Airport

Rustenburg

## FACILITIES

All Hides and Picnic Spots are equipped with toilets and are safely fenced. Picnic Spots also offer braai facilities, water and shade. Most Points of Discovery and Viewsites do not have facilities and are not fenced. Please do not get out unless the area is fenced and it is safe to do so.

## SHADED RELIEF

Metres above mean sea level

Matlhorwe (1687m)

Maritane (1397m)

Mankwe Dam (1120m)

1660 1630 1600 1570 1540 1510 1480 1450 1420 1390 1360 1330 1300 1270 1240 1210 1180 1150 1120 1090 1060 1030

# POINTS OF DISCOVERY

Discovering Pilanesberg can be more than just a glimpse of one, two, or (if you are lucky) three of the Big Five. The Map will help you find unusual and interesting features that you may have otherwise overlooked. From the fascinating world of insects, to magical and medicinal trees, these Discovery Points provide the clues as to where … and why … and how it all happens in Pilanesberg.

## Please note as you drive along:

- The Discovery Points are not necessarily in numerical order.
- Not all points are right next to the road. Look around carefully where the point is marked.
- Some numbers are repeated at more than one place in the Park.
- Geological sites (G1-15) are indicated with their relevant rock colours corresponding to the map on page 4.

## 1 Manyane Complex

### North West Parks & Tourism Board Headquarters
E-mail: nwptb@iafrica.com
Web: www.tourismnorthwest.co.za
Tel: (014) 555-5351/2/3/4   Fax: (014) 555-5525

## 2 Walking Area (Self-guided Trails)
Stretch your legs and enjoy nature at close range, by experiencing the Walking Area at Manyane. This area is fenced and has no large, dangerous animals. A route map and guide to interesting features is available. This offers environmental education while enjoying game viewing or bird watching on foot.

*Lebibi, see page 23*

## 4 Bushveld Shepherds-tree Area
The unusual *Boscia foetida* or 'Stinkwitgat' is drought resistant. It gets its name from the pungent smell of the flowers and inner wood. The edible fruit tastes like capers.

*Motlopi, see page 21*

## 6 Management Sites
Throughout the Park you can see efforts to curb erosion, help rehabilitate over-used areas and create attractive sites. Silt traps, weirs, dams, gabions and rock packs are some examples of management control.

### Manyane
- Self-catering and time share chalets
- Caravan park with 100 fully-electrified caravan stands, 60 camping sites, ablution & laundry facilities
- A lá carte restaurant, shop & bar
- Swimming pool, jungle gym, mini-golf and walk-in aviary (over 80 species of indigenous birds)
- Bosele Camp with dormitories; fully catered (for school groups of up to 204 children)

Tel: (014) 555-6135/9   Fax: (014) 555-6122

### Mankwe Safaris
- Offer game drives, walks and bush braais
- Specialise in heritage drives with particular focus on the Tswana culture

Tel: (014) 555-7056   Fax: (014) 555-7884

### Pilanesberg Safaris
- Game drives, walks and bush braais
- Hot air balloons

Tel: (014) 555-5469   Fax: (014) 555-5684

## 3 Salty Spring
A mineral hotspot that provides animals with vital nutrients all year long.

## 5 Volcanic Tuff G1
1 300 million years ago a volcanic eruption blasted massive rocks, kilometres into the sky. The biggest boulders fell back to earth first; smaller ones scattered at random above them. A series of blasts, over time, created layers of these rocks, called tuffs. Erosion has exposed them to us.

THE OLD MAN OF MORULENG

*Leave only your tracks.*
*Take only your photographs.*
*Please do not litter*
*or pick anything.*

## 7 Malatse Hide – Fenced

A site showing management's efforts to restore nature and to provide visitors with rewarding viewing. The weir and man-made dam prevent erosion and have encouraged wildlife back to this dry part of the Park. Sable, eland and rhino may be among the rewards for patient viewers.

## 8 Nepheline Syenite G2

This rock was formed when boiling magma rose to just below the earth's surface. Here it cooled down rapidly and solidified. White feldspar crystals were captured in the direction of the flowing magma.

## 9 Gully Thickets

Remnants of ancient forests survive where two hillsides meet. These gullies collect water and soil, and the denser vegetation provides good habitat for leopard, bushbuck, kudu and a wealth of forest birds.

## 10 Bakgatla

- Manyane style brick chalets set in attractive mountains
- Full facilities & swimming pool
- Braai & picnic sites with kiosk, ablutions & children's playground
- Camp site

**Tel: (014) 555-6135/9  Fax: (014) 555-6122**

## 11 Ratlhogo Hide – Fenced

An excellent hide to watch game coming down to drink, mud-rollers (like warthog) enjoying a wallow, terrapin and birds. The karee trees are indicative of wet areas. Thick bush provides good cover for kudu, bushbuck, waterbuck and other woodland species.

*Kolobe ya Naga, see page 33*

## 12 Lava G3

As lava flowed on the earth's surface, it cooled rapidly through exposure to air and wind.

## 14 Kimberlite G4

In the 1920s a fortune-seeking prospector discovered this Kimberlite pipe. The bright red garnets he found here could have indicated diamonds; so he dug in excitement, but in vain!

## 13 Soil Formation

Large boulders tumble down from the hills, eventually crumbling into soil. The ongoing process of soil formation takes thousands of years. This process is easy to see in hundreds of places in Pilanesberg.

## 16 Lesser Masked Weaver Colony

When full or during the rainy season, weavers flock to this water habitat for safety and food. Man-made dams often create new habitats for many species.

## 15 Tamboti Circle

Black Rhino and porcupine enjoy these highly poisonous trees, but smoke of burning wood causes nausea and headaches in humans. In Nov-Jan look out for tamboti 'jumping beans' – the caterpillars of a small grey moth spasmodically stretching inside the tamboti seeds.

*Morukuru, see page 30*

*Thaga, see page 31*

## Points of discovery

### 17 Marula Area

The magic marula means food, drink, medicine and myth in Africa. It is traditionally used to treat colds, dysentery, diarrhoea, and as an anti-histamine; also to increase fertility in women.

*Marula, see page 17*

*We must be careful not to start fires – never throw cigarettes or matches into the veld.*

THE OLD MAN OF MORULENG

### 18 Rock Figs

Look high on the cliffside to see the *Ficus* species taking root in rocks, splitting them with their geotropic (earth-seeking) force. Their white roots are distinctive on many rocky areas throughout the Park.

*Moumo, see page 24*

### 19 Live-long Lannea

The *Lannea discolor* a single-trunked tree branching into a few thick branches that spread to form a sparse, irregular canopy. It is said to cure fever and constipation. Poles, fishing floats and twine are made from it.

*Mmotshwana, see page 12*

### 20 Uranium-bearing Rock

This rock is a continuation of G13 (Point 25) on the other side of the hill. Such 'spurs' can go on for miles underground, being exposed through erosion at some points.

### 21 Flat Rock and Natural Seep

A natural seep causes permanent water to collect and attracts game to this area.

### 22 Resurrection Plant

A hardy plant that appears dead in dry times, but a little water brings it to miraculous life.

*Moswiarula, see page 25*

### 23 Termite Mounds

These small, rounded mounds have been created by the genus *Hodotermes*. This is the first step to rehabilitation, as termites eat the dead wood from felled trees, and soon birds and game return to lengthen the food chain.

### 24 Black Eagle Nest

A pair of Verreaux's Eagles (formerly known as Black Eagles) breed up on the cliffs. These eagles pair for life, and can sometimes be seen in flight or perched on rocks.

*Ntsu, see page 27*

### 25 Uranium-bearing Tuff G13

These tuffs (see Point 5) are mildly radioactive due to their uranium content. The minerals in these rocks are a result of super-heated water (200-400°C) which soaked into the rock at the end of the volcanoes' active life.

## 26 Black-thorn Acacia Area

Indicative of nutritious Sweetveld, these *Acacia mellifera* trees are excellent fodder for browsers. Grass is sometimes lacking in Sweetveld as it is well utilized by grazers. In old times, these trees were used to form kraals or to snare fish driven down a narrow stream.

*Mongana, see page 22*

## 27 Fish Eagle Nest

For many years this has been home to a pair of African Fish Eagles. Like the Verreaux's Eagle, these birds mate for life. They live in a fiercely defended territory and often return to the same nest for generations. Look in the wooded area, quite far off the road in the tall, dead tree.

*Kgoadira, see page 30*

## 28 Weeping Faurea (Transvaal Beech)

These fire-resistant trees are indicative of Sourveld which does not provide much nutrition in winter. Due to the accumulation of dry, unpalatable grasses, Sourveld burns very easily. A red dye is made from these *Faurea saligna* trees.

*Mofufu, see page 23*

## 29 Red Syenite G7

This makes good polished facing stone. Twenty years ago attempts to quarry it failed as it contains small, yellow grains of iron oxide which do not polish well. On the hill behind this site, long, vertical, drilling holes can be seen (see Point 67).

## 30 Bushveld Red-balloon

This extremely rare plant, *Erythrophysa transvaalensis*, occurs only in syenite koppies. It can be seen above the drilled rocks at G7 (Point 29), growing almost out of the rock. This tree is protected in South Africa.

## 31 Mankwe Lake View Platform – Fenced

Situated in the centre of Pilanesberg, this spot offers excellent viewing, especially of waterbirds. The domed hills bear testament to volcanic activity, pushed out through plugs in the earth's crust. Crocodile and hippo rule the water and birds come to breed and feed nearby.

## 32 White Foyaite G5

The surrounding hills are white foyaite, a coarse-grained rock that crystallised slowly from molten magma inside the earth. It is rich in minerals, like feldspar and nepheline and the rare metal, zirconium (see Points 35 and 38).

## 33 Animal Off-loading Ramp

In 1979 this ramp was used extensively in "Operation Genesis", the largest translocation of game to date. The many species of game introduced into the park have flourished over the past 22 years.

## 35 White Foyaite G14

Foyaites are not easily weathered. This explains why the hills in this area are prominent (see Points 32 and 38).

## 34 Naboom (Euphorbia)

A cactus-like plant, the *Euphorbia ingens*, is enjoyed by Black Rhino. The San used it to make poison arrows and its milky latex can blind people. Some say the tree is a protection against lightning. They are often home to genets and bushbabies.

*Ngoge, see page 24*

## 36 Fish Eagle Picnic Site – Fenced

The superb view, variety of trees, distinctive rocks and the interface of 3 habitats (rocky outcrop, hillside and water) make this attractive area a haven for wildlife. It was once a kraal site, being easily defendable and close to water. Trees include *Acacias*, bushwillows, tamboti and marula.

THE OLD MAN OF MORULENG

*It is dangerous to get out of your car except at fenced sites, like picnic spots, hides, camps and lodges.*

## Points of discovery

### 37 Bakubung

*LEGACY HOTELS & RESORTS*

- Superb hotel accommodation overlooking private dam with resident hippos
- Bar area, restaurant, curio shop, conference centre & sporting facilities
- Afternoon, sunrise & sundowner game drives & bush braais
- Guided bush trails

**Tel: (014) 552-6000  Fax: (014) 552-6161**

### 38 Green Foyaite G10

There are several varieties of foyaite with similar compositions, but differing proportions of minerals. The nepheline in this rock dissolves easily resulting in a pitted surface typical of the foyaites (see Point 53).

### 39 Wagon Tracks

From a century ago these tracks have left their mark in the ouklip rock. Ouklip is formed when water evaporates leaving minerals behind. On the other side of the road on the far slope, are lines of trees – evidence of an old orchard. Indigenous trees have taken advantage of the old orchard holes.

### 40 Old Fluorite Mine G8

The old Moepo mine can be seen up against the mountain, where purple fluorite, containing calcium and fluorine, was mined. These minerals soaked into the rocks in the same way that mineralisation happened at Point 25.

### 41 Browser and Bird Area

Stop, look, listen and smell. Often a rewarding area for birds and browsers who come to woody areas for food and safety (see pages 18 - 23).

*LEGACY HOTELS & RESORTS*

### 42 TSHUKUDU

- 6 luxury thatched chalets, nestled against an isolated koppie and overlooking its own waterhole with superb game viewing
- Game drives and walks accompanied by a ranger
- Five star standards

**Tel: (014) 552-6255**
**Fax: (014) 552-6266**

### 43 Brown Hyaena Area

These shy, nocturnal animals are seldom seen, but keep a sharp lookout, especially on a night drive, because their lair is hidden nearby in the safety of the rocky hillsides. White middens (heaps of dung used as territorial markers) may often be seen next to the road.

*Phiri, see page 37*

### 44 Common Protea (Highveld Protea)

This sugarbush (*Protea caffra*) was depicted on the old South African 3 and 6 penny coins. Flowers Nov-Feb.

## 45 Ruighoek Dam

A natural catchment area, surrounded by 4 prominent habitats – water, hillside, grassland and woodland. As a result many species occur, especially those dependent on water. A wide variety of trees including Karee, African Olive, Shepherds-tree and Buffalo-thorn Jujube make this an excellent area for birds and game.

## 46 Buffalo Area

Pilanesberg buffalo were introduced from Addo Elephant National Park as they were free of foot and mouth, and Corridor disease. To keep the herds healthy, buffalo from other regions will not be introduced. Look out for them in these areas.

*Nare, see page 17*

## 47 Moepel (Transvaal Red Milkwood)

This milkwood, *Mimusops zeyheri,* has simple glossy, dark lime-green leaves. The leaves and the orange-yellow fruit are enjoyed by elephants, baboons, kudu, duiker and fruit-eating birds. The wood is used to make farm implements.

## 48 Geographic Centre G15

This is the approximate geographic centre of the volcano. There are multiple, parallel bands of syenite and red foyaite, created over a million years ago from magma. This site is underwater for many months of the year.

## 49 Makorwane Dam – Hide

Another diversity of habitat with grassland, hills, rocky outcrops and water. Primary grassland and sweet thorn trees are the first stage of indigenous vegetation re-establishing on old farmlands. Note aloes on the hill and flooded trees which are good nesting sites. Dams help to recreate well-balanced water habitats.

## 50 Pilanesberg Centre

*Pilanesberg Centre*

Built in 1936 as a Magistrate's Court, the Pilanesberg Centre has been converted into a restaurant and curio shop. Enjoy breakfast, lunch or tea from the terrace of this finely preserved building.
**Tel: 083 378 1080**

## 51 Graveyard

This graveyard dates back to the 1930s, and is still visited by descendants of the family. It is Park policy not to remove old graves.

THE OLD MAN OF MORULENG

*Animals have the right of way, so please do not exceed 40 km/h and keep on the road.*

## Points of discovery

### 52 Lenong View

Named after the vulture, this panoramic view sheds light on the Pilanesberg volcano. The mountains were once boiling magma, pushed up through concentric cracks in the earth's crust. These are called ring dykes, exposed to us through weathering. Scars of old farmland are evident in erosion and open, recovering grassland. Natural processes assisted by management rehabilitate the area. The mountain top is Sourveld where Weeping Faurea, Resurrection Plant, Highveld Protea and Rock Figs grow. Mountain Reedbuck, eland and gemsbok can be found here.

### 53 Green Foyaite G6

In the surging sea of magma, deep below the earths' surface, many minerals were carried upwards. As the magma cooled they became set into rock. One of them is aegerine, which grew in a needle-like form in this green foyaite (see Point 38).

### 54 Reedbuck Area

Rewarding to see as they are shy and rare, Common Reedbuck are dependent on water and can be seen at vleis. Look out for Mountain Reedbuck on these hills.

*Motlobo, see page 28*

### 55 Macrotermes Termite Mound

This mound has been created by the genus *Macrotermes*. This termite is renowned for building extremely large mounds, some of which are taller than 1,8 m. These termites contribute to the ecosystem by advancing the decomposition process of dead wood.

### 56 Old Farmhouse Foundations

These are the remains of the farmhouse of one of the families that lived and farmed on the land. Most signs of farming activities were removed in the late '70s.

### 57 Moloto Picinic – Fenced

Mountains and rocky outcrops are home to baboon, klipspringer, leopard and large raptors. Good grassl and nearby is where buffalo, reedbuck, giraffe and lion can be seen. This interface of 2 habitats draws a wide variety of species, especially birds.

### 58 Red Foyaite G9

The rugged country in this area is underlain by white foyaite. The red foyaite was created when super-heated water altered the composition and colour of the rock, through soaking it with red iron oxide.

### 59 Moloto Plain

A spectacular view of grasslands, rocky outcrops, hillsides, water and woodlands. Animals like White Rhino, wildebeest, springbok, zebra and cheetah can be seen on the plain. A wide variety of trees germinate and seed easily in rocky areas where water and soil collect.

### 60 Rhino Rubbing Post

Some posts in the Park are smooth from years of White Rhino enjoying a good rub to remove parasites from their skin.

## 61 Church Site

This is a Dutch Reformed Church site, dating from 1964. The African Olive trees were used to treat colic, sore eyes and throats. See also the Buffalo-thorn Jujube, a sacred tree to the Zulu people.

## 62 White Rhino Middens

White Rhino use this site as a territorial marker.
Having stepped in the dung, the rhino walks his territory, ensuring it is well scented. Dung beetles frequent these middens, laying eggs in the dung balls. The hatched grubs are eaten by birds, baboons, genets and civets, creating a long food chain in nature.

## 63 *Kwa Maritane* Place of the Rock

- Luxurious hotel & timeshare game lodge, 5 bed luxury duplex cabanas or 8 bed chalets with private patios
- Conference centre, bar & restaurant overlooking illuminated waterhole
- Underground viewing hide
- Two swimming pools; tennis and volleyball courts
- Day and night game drives; bush braais

**Tel: (014) 552-5100**
**Fax: (014) 552-5333**

## 64 Ledig Foyaite G11

This contains small, unharmful amounts of uranium, as well as aegerine (magnesium, iron, sodium and silica).
It is also formed from magma.

## 65 Iron Age Walling

Walls can be seen throughout Pilanesberg. They date back to the 17th Century when Batswana settlements sprung up throughout the Western Transvaal. Small villages were built at the base of hills so that look-outs could be easily posted without enemies detecting the village. Some may even have belonged to the infamous Matabele chief, Mzilikaze.

## 66 Klipspringer Koppie

This is a favoured area for this unusual antelope whose sure-footed hooves can cling to steep rock. The klipspringer, found throughout Africa, can live independently of water.

## 67 Red Syenite G12

Different from the syenite at 29, this is largely composed of potassium-rich orthoclase, feldspar, chlorite (iron, magnesium, silica and water), calcium and fluorine. Syenite is igneous rock, meaning it formed from magma.

(58)

# SPECIES TICK LIST

The following grids are for you to tick off your discoveries of plants, birds, mammals, reptiles and insects.

These have been set out with four columns so that you can keep separate counts on different days… or in different seasons… or on different trips…

Enjoy the discovery of finding it in Pilanesberg!

GRASSES

| Page No. | SHRUBS | | | |
|---|---|---|---|---|
| 32 | Black-jack | | | |
| 26 | Fern, Hard | | | |
| 32 | Khaki Weed | | | |
| 27 | Lichen | | | |
| 26 | Mother-in-law's Tongue | | | |
| 33 | Nightshade | | | |
| 20 | Num-num, Forest | | | |
| 22 | Puzzle Bush Stamperwood | | | |
| 26 | Raisin Bush | | | |
| 25 | Resurrection Plant | | | |
| 19 | Spike-thorn, Kraal | | | |

| Page No. | TREES | | | |
|---|---|---|---|---|
| 13 | Aloe, Mountain | | | |
| 28 | Broad-pod Elephant-root | | | |
| 22 | Black-thorn Acacia | | | |
| 19 | Buffalo-thorn Jujube | | | |
| 21 | Bushveld Shepherds-tree | | | |
| 12 | Bushwillow, Large-fruit | | | |
| 14 | Leadwood | | | |
| 12 | Red | | | |
| 28 | River | | | |
| 12 | Velvet-leaved | | | |
| 24 | Cabbage-tree | | | |
| 24 | Fig, Large-leaved Rock | | | |
| 18 | Jacket-plum | | | |
| 28 | Karee | | | |
| 26 | Lavender Croton | | | |
| 12 | Live-long Lannea | | | |
| 17 | Marula | | | |
| 24 | Naboom | | | |
| 18 | Olive, African | | | |
| 22 | Puzzle-bush Stamperwood | | | |
| 16 | Sweet-thorn Acacia | | | |
| 30 | Tamboti | | | |
| 16 | Umbrella Acacia | | | |
| 14 | Wattle, African Weeping- | | | |
| 23 | Weeping Faurea | | | |
| 26 | Wild-pear Dombeya | | | |

| Page No. | GRASSES/REEDS | | | |
|---|---|---|---|---|
| 35 | Blue Buffalo | | | |
| 24 | Bristle-leaved Red Top | | | |
| 25 | Common Russet | | | |
| 34 | Couch | | | |
| 32 | Feathered Chloris | | | |
| 17 | Fine Thatching | | | |
| 29 | Finger | | | |
| 13 | Golden Beard | | | |
| 18 | Guinea | | | |
| 17 | Gum | | | |
| 12 | Hairy Blue | | | |
| 15 | Narrow-leaved Turpentine | | | |
| 33 | Natal Red Top | | | |
| 31 | Reeds | | | |
| 27 | Silky Bushman | | | |
| 28 | Sorghum, Common Wild | | | |
| 16 | White Buffalo | | | |
| 15 | Wire | | | |
| 16 | Wool | | | |

INSECTS

| Page No. | INSECTS | | | |
|---|---|---|---|---|
| 32 | Ants | | | |
| 32 | Beetle, Dung | | | |
| 36 | Cricket, Common | | | |
| 28 | Dragonfly, Emperor | | | |
| 27 | Fly, Robber | | | |
| 32 | Millipede | | | |
| 36 | Moth, Death's Head Hawk | | | |
| 36 | Looper | | | |
| 36 | Praying Mantis | | | |
| 21 | Spider, Garbage Line | | | |
| 18 | Golden Brown Baboon | | | |
| 21 | Golden Orb Web | | | |
| 18 | Tropical Tent | | | |
| 24 | Wall Crab | | | |
| 16 | Termites, Snouted | | | |
| 24 | Tick, Hard | | | |

REPTILES

| Page No. | REPTILES | | | |
|---|---|---|---|---|
| 32 | Adder, Puff | | | |
| 26 | Agama, Southern rock | | | |
| 29 | Crocodile, Nile | | | |
| 28 | Frog, Foam nest | | | |
| 28 | Striped Stream | | | |
| 21 | Gecko, Tropical house | | | |
| 26 | Mamba, Black | | | |
| 26 | Monitor, Rock | | | |
| 28 | Water | | | |
| 26 | Python, African rock | | | |
| 36 | Skink, Common striped | | | |
| 18 | Snake, Spotted bush | | | |
| 28 | Terrapin, Cape | | | |
| 20 | Toad, Red | | | |
| 32 | Tortoise, Leopard | | | |

BIRDS

## Tips for spotting

- The best times for game spotting are the early mornings and the late afternoons.
- Sit in a shady spot and wait patiently – like animals do.
- Listen and watch carefully.
- For best viewing drive at 20 km/h.

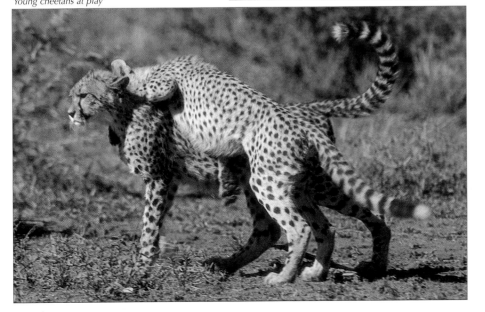

*Young cheetahs at play*

| Page No. | BIRDS | | | |
|---|---|---|---|---|
| 20 | Babbler, Arrow-marked | | | |
| 12 | Southern Pied | | | |
| 20 | Barbet, Black-collared | | | |
| 12 | Crested | | | |
| 23 | Batis, Chinspot | | | |
| 33 | Bee-eater, Little | | | |
| 33 | White-fronted | | | |
| 22 | Bulbul, Dark-capped | | | |
| 32 | Bunting, Golden-breasted | | | |
| 32 | Rock | | | |
| 34 | Bustard, Kori | | | |
| 27 | Chat, Mocking | | | |
| 30 | Cormorant, White-breasted | | | |
| 30 | Darter, African | | | |
| 36 | Dikkop, Spotted | | | |
| 20 | Dove, Cape Turtle | | | |
| 20 | Emerald-spotted | | | |
| 20 | Laughing | | | |
| 22 | Drongo, Fork-tailed | | | |
| 30 | Duck, White-faced | | | |
| 31 | Yellow-billed | | | |
| 31 | Eagle, African Fish | | | |
| 17 | Black-chested Snake | | | |
| 34 | Tawny | | | |
| 27 | Verreaux's | | | |
| 34 | Wahlberg's | | | |
| 16 | Egret, Cattle | | | |
| 22 | Firefinch, Jameson's | | | |
| 22 | Red-billed | | | |
| 23 | Flycatcher, Marico | | | |

| Page No. | BIRDS (continued) | | | |
|---|---|---|---|---|
| 32 | Francolin, Coqui | | | |
| 32 | Crested | | | |
| 32 | Natal | | | |
| 30 | Goose, Egyptian | | | |
| 30 | Spur-winged | | | |
| 30 | Grebe, Little | | | |
| 20 | Guineafowl, Helmeted | | | |
| 30 | Hamerkop | | | |
| 31 | Heron, Grey | | | |
| 22 | Hoopoe, African | | | |
| 20 | Hornbill, Red-billed | | | |
| 20 | Southern Yellow-billed | | | |
| 31 | Ibis, Hadeda | | | |
| 27 | Kestrel, Common | | | |
| 23 | Kingfisher, Brown-hooded | | | |
| 31 | Pied | | | |
| 23 | Striped | | | |
| 16 | Kite, Black-shouldered | | | |
| 34 | Korhaan, Red-crested | | | |
| 34 | Southern Black | | | |
| 13 | Lark, Rufous-naped | | | |
| 13 | Sabota | | | |
| 23 | Loerie, Grey | | | |
| 27 | Martin, Rock | | | |
| 23 | Mousebird, Speckled | | | |
| 23 | White-backed | | | |
| 36 | Nightjars | | | |
| 22 | Oriole, Black-headed | | | |
| 35 | Ostrich | | | |
| 36 | Owl, Pearl-spotted | | | |
| 36 | Spotted Eagle | | | |
| 20 | Pigeon, Rock | | | |
| 31 | Plover, Three-banded | | | |
| 16 | Roller, Lilac-breasted | | | |
| 20 | Scrub-Robin, White-browed | | | |
| 35 | Secretarybird | | | |
| 22 | Shrike, Crimson-breasted | | | |
| 22 | Common Fiscal | | | |
| 32 | Spurfowl, Swainson's | | | |
| 20 | Starling, Cape Glossy | | | |
| 27 | Red-winged | | | |
| 30 | Swallow, White-throated | | | |
| 34 | Vulture, Cape | | | |
| 34 | Lappet-faced | | | |
| 34 | White-backed | | | |
| 23 | Waxbill, Blue | | | |
| 31 | Weaver, Lesser Masked | | | |
| 16 | Whydah, Pin-tailed | | | |
| 22 | Wood-Hoopoe, Green | | | |
| 22 | Woodpecker, Cardinal | | | |

MAMMALS

| Page No. | MAMMALS | | | |
|---|---|---|---|---|
| 36 | Aardvark | | | |
| 37 | Aardwolf | | | |
| 13 | Antelope, Sable | | | |
| 24 | Baboon, Chacma | | | |
| 17 | Buffalo | | | |
| 37 | Bushbaby, Lesser | | | |
| 19 | Bushbuck | | | |
| 37 | Caracal | | | |
| 14 | Cheetah | | | |
| 36 | Civet, African | | | |
| 25 | Dassie, Rock | | | |
| 18 | Duiker, Common | | | |
| 12 | Eland | | | |
| 21 | Elephant | | | |
| 13 | Gemsbok | | | |
| 36 | Genet, Large-spotted | | | |
| 21 | Giraffe | | | |
| 37 | Hare, Scrub | | | |
| 34 | Korhaan, Black | | | |
| 14 | Hartebeest, Red | | | |
| 29 | Hippopotamus | | | |
| 37 | Hyaena, Brown | | | |
| 19 | Impala | | | |
| 14 | Jackal, Black-backed | | | |
| 24 | Klipspringer | | | |
| 12 | Kudu | | | |
| 25 | Leopard | | | |
| 15 | Lion | | | |
| 33 | Ostrich | | | |
| 36 | Mongoose, Slender | | | |
| 18 | Monkey, Vervet | | | |
| 36 | Porcupine | | | |
| 28 | Reedbuck, Common | | | |
| 12 | Mountain | | | |
| 19 | Rhinoceros, Black | | | |
| 15 | White | | | |
| 14 | Springbok | | | |
| 18 | Squirrel, Tree | | | |
| 18 | Steenbok | | | |
| 14 | Tssessebe | | | |
| 33 | Warthog | | | |
| 29 | Waterbuck, Common | | | |
| 15 | Wildebeest, Blue | | | |
| 13 | Zebra, Plains | | | |

# INDEX